Albany Island

Old Crater

James Bay

High

Green

Mountains

Lava Flow

Goya Rico

Salt Lake

Conway

Spring

German Grafi

Spring

Sugar Loaf Mt.

nama

Colombia

Quito
Ecuador
Guayaquil

Peru

1 mile

SANTIAGO

J. Brady

RETURN TO THE ISLAND

By AINSLIE & FRANCES CONWAY

THE ENCHANTED ISLANDS

Second Edition.   *Illustrated.*   15s net

"Mrs. Conway, whose photograph in the book shows her smiling, smiled all through their long adventure. She can also make her readers smile through the years she and her husband spent building houses, clearing the jungle that food might grow and resisting invasions by donkeys, pigs and wild bulls. How Robinson Crusoe would have laughed at those who chose to put themselves on a desert island for the fun of it!"

—*The Times Literary Supplement.*

"*The Enchanted Islands* is a lively account of the authors' difficult but evidently enjoyable life in this remarkable group of islands, inhabited not merely by tortoises but by Ecuadorians, criminals, and an international assortment of derelicts and idealists."

—*The Sunday Times.*

"The authors write with a wit as sturdy as their determination to live where they want, and although the book may make no converts to their kind of pioneering, it does provide entertainment."

—*Sphere.*

"*The Enchanted Islands* is something new in the literature of escape."

—*John o' London's Weekly.*

AINSLIE AND FRANCES CONWAY

RETURN
TO THE ISLAND

by
AINSLIE & FRANCES CONWAY

LONDON
GEOFFREY BLES
1952

Printed in Great Britain by
Wyman & Sons, Ltd., Fakenham
for Geoffrey Bles, Ltd.
52 Doughty Street, London, W.C.1

First published 1952

To

ROSALINE AND CLARENCE FISHER

and

THE GOAT-WHISKERED GALÁPAGANS

CONTENTS

ILLUSTRATIONS

The drawings in the text are by Frances Conway

* *Photographs by* H. R. TEGENS
The other photographs by ALLAN HANCOCK FOUNDATION

I. AINSLIE HANGS MOROS AND I EAT BLOOD

The sun had set over Guayaquil. The lights were coming on. The brightest light shone above the white-washed statue of Cristo on the highest spire of the tallest cathedral in the city. Against the purple clouds of evening the spire and its high-placed guardian looked magnificent. But we who had lived in a crowded hotel under their shadow and illumination for two months discounted the illusion. The cathedral was an old termite-riddled shell of wood and bamboo and corrugated iron —as much of it as had ever been completed—and the light failed at least once a week.

The *Abdón Calderón*, venerable Ecuadorian gunboat, was docked for taking on oil. She was gunboat in name only, for she had no gun, and the oil was measured exactly for a trip to four of the Galápagos Islands and return and not one engine's turn farther. The dock was near the municipal slaughter-house on the bank of the Guayas Estuary. During the day *gallinazos* had lined themselves by the hundreds on the ridgepoles of the abattoir and adjoining buildings. In the fading twilight we could see them sitting and waiting.

We watched the bright light of salvation and the black birds of doom and were bored. And tired. And in pain. We had been aboard the *Calderón* since noon, the hour *en punto* when she was scheduled to pull out, stared at by the full sun, glared at by his reflection in the water. With a dozen other first-class passengers we were parked on the after-deck, which had once had an awning—as the ship had also once had a gun—but the awning had worn out during the war and a new one was thus far only a plan and a promise. Like the *gallinazos* we were waiting— waiting for the commander to come aboard.

Suddenly there was a horrid commotion behind us. Coming to life and wheeling around was an immediate impulse. The next was stepping back to avoid the spurting blood. No, it was not spurting yet, but the signs said that bloody action was imminent. I was wearing a white shirt and blue slacks and did not care to have my sea-going colour scheme ruined. The other passengers must have stepped back too, for an open space appeared on the boards and in the centre of it stood a smartly-uniformed bantam rooster, his face red with fury. The commander had come aboard.

"Get off my ship at once!" he yelled, as the veins on his temples filled to bursting.

Standing in front of him was a copper-faced seaman in a petty officer's cap, his shoulders hunched and his head bowed. "I will not get off," he said in level, stubborn tones. "*Mi comandante*, I want to go to the Galápagos."

"Get off my ship, I say!" repeated the commander, shaking his clenched fists above his head. "I give the orders."

"I will not get off, *mi comandante*," repeated the seaman, holding his clenched fists tight against his faded jeans. "I want to go to the Galápagos."

"I say, get off——!" the commander screamed, but he could not finish the sentence. His voice cracked. He swallowed with difficulty. "Guard!" he barked. "Guard, come here!"

A teen-age guard, dressed in white shorts and white cap and nothing more, marched up and saluted. A yard of sword blade hung in a scabbard at his hip.

Before the guard had completed his salute, the commander had jerked him around and snatched the sword from the scabbard, and was waving the wicked old blade in a wide arc. "I say, get off my ship!" he screamed again.

The seaman stood impassive. "Run me through with the sword, *mi comandante*," he said in the same cool, stubborn voice, "riddle my belly with bullets. But I will not get off. I want to go to the Galápagos."

The sword whistled in the air above the *comandante*'s head and closer to the passengers pressed against the rail. He opened his mouth to scream once more. Only a small, mewling sound issued. His loose upper plate had fallen down on the lower.

The little commander's suffused face grew pale. He clapped his free hand over his mouth and seemed to chew and swallow. Quickly he gave the sword to the guard. "Take this man to the guardhouse," he ordered.

As the guard marched the seaman away, the commander stood still for a moment, straightened his cap, curled his moustache, adjusted his expression to one of dignity and authority, and finally dusted his hands on a white handkerchief. "Let's go!" he said to the executive officer, who had been standing by in rapt admiration. Then with his shoulders held very square and his stride lengthened to the limit of his little legs, the *comandante* marched up on the bridge.

Presently the ship began to move down the estuary. The tide was at flood, and certainly it was time. As I watched the light of Cristo recede, I wondered what had happened to the one-man-mutiny. A half-hour later a seaman passed by unconcernedly. It was the mutineer himself. "What was the trouble a while ago?" I asked.

"There was no trouble," he answered without glancing at me.

"Serves you right," Ainslie told me. "You should know better than to ask."

"Doesn't matter, I guess. For, after all, he is going to the Galápagos. And so are we, it seems—again."

Just like that, in the year 1937, we had picked up our suitcases and our last five hundred dollars and shipped off toward the Galápagos Islands. Now the Galápagos are a long way from San Francisco, where the first lap of our journey had begun, and even at depression prices more than half of our capital had gone down the spout before we had reached Guayaquil, Ecuador, which is the jumping-off place for the islands. It had taken two

hundred dollars more to get tickets for the little island boat
and buy supplies and equipment. One does not go to the
Galápagos without taking along food, tools, and building
materials—not if one is also taking along one's right mind and
expects to live in the islands indefinitely. Even the four inhabited islands are still considered "desert," and the island of
our choice, Santiago, was, and is, both desert and uninhabited.
Moreover, recent volcanic activity had been observed on the
island, and the Ecuadorians, who own the Galápagos, were
afraid of it.

We have told the story of that first Galápagos venture in a
previous book, *The Enchanted Islands*. In our lexicon the word
"enchanted" means "accursed," and it meant the same in the
lexicons of the Spanish adventurers who discovered the archipelago in the sixteenth century and called it "Las Islas
Encantadas." We tell you this so you won't get starry-eyed.
Many people when they come upon the word "enchanted" at
once take off mentally to some houri-infested Paradise.

Our spellbound islands rise out of the deep sea bottom six
hundred miles straight west from the coast of Ecuador, and they
are hung on the equatorial line like Mother Johnson's Monday
wash. They are volcanic relics of a long-lost age when reptiles
and birds were the world's first families. On modern maps the
island group is named for the noblest reptiles of the region—the
giant tortoises or galápagos, which once covered the islands
almost shell to shell but are now nearly extinct. They have
been replaced by donkeys, goats, hogs, and cattle which run
wild over most of the islands. These latter-day animals are
descendants of herds abandoned by pirates, whalers, and early
settlers who came years ago and failed to stay.

In the early nineteenth century Ecuador claimed the archipelago because no one else wanted it, and named it "El
Archipiélago de Colón" just to put a note of decent formality
into the ceremony of taking over. That no other nation wanted
it was rather strange. British and American whalers had used
the islands as bases of operation for the better part of a century
—one reason why there are few galápagos left—and some colourful engagements of the war of 1812 had been fought on the
surrounding waters. The British Admiralty had also charted
the islands and given them names. The British, who have
claimed all sorts of islands all over the world, must have thought
there was something very, very wrong about the Galápagos.
There is.

Many of the Galápagos islands, especially the smaller ones of low altitude, are all but waterless and therefore uninhabitable. Four of these heaps of lava, slag, and volcanic ash, large enough in the case of Isabela to reach a length of seventy-five miles and an altitude of over four thousand feet, have been settled by Ecuadorians and a few dozen Europeans. The Galápagos never had any so-called natives. The inhabited islands are Isabela (Albermarle), San Cristóbal (Chatham), Santa Cruz (Indefatigable), and Floreana (Santa María or Charles). The first settlers were "exiled" convicts from Ecuador, who were already in possession of Floreana in 1835, when Darwin came to study the odd fauna of the place. They were there under the patronage of General Valdizián, who was raising tobacco and cattle and gathering a special kind of moss which flourishes in the damp higher regions of the archipelago. Valdizián was later murdered by his convict-labourers, and the prison settlement was moved to San Cristóbal, where the *padrón*, Manuel J. Cobos, was also murdered. During the last war, Villamil, at Isabela, became the home of the convict colony. Also during the last war, the United States built an air base on Baltra Island, which is an arm of Santa Cruz broken off in some dreadful volcanic upheaval long ago.

Our first stay in the Galápagos had lasted four and a half years for me and six years for Ainslie. At the beginning of the late war I had returned to California, to do my bit, and Ainslie—the perennial soldier, whether in the army or out—had stayed on to help build the air base on Baltra. Of that time we had spent three months on the virgin Santiago (San Salvador or James), where we had first landed, and then had been evacuated by the Ecuadorian government, without our blessing, to Floreana. Santiago, the government had said, was not safe nor habitable.

We were soon reconciled to Floreana, for it is one of the most picturesque and colourful of the islands and has harboured some of their most interesting settlers: Dr. Friedrich Ritter and Dore Strauch, who as latter-day Adam and Eve were publicised by the Press in the 1930's, and Baroness Eloise Bousquet von Wagner and her retinue of lovers, who were Ritter's contemporaries. In 1934 Dr. Ritter died "under mysterious circumstances" and the Baroness and her best boy friend "disappeared" under "mysterious circumstances." Since then the Galápagos have been identified in most people's minds as the stamping grounds of those characters, and at least two books and who knows how many articles have been written about them. No news-purveying sheet, not excluding *Time Magazine*, can mention the islands without dragging in the unfortunate Baroness Eloise by the seat of her pink silk panties, which, according to news writers, made up her favourite costume. Something about those panties. By them we are dragging her in, too.

Among the more "solid" Floreana citizens, perhaps a dozen at present, are the German Wittmers, who have lived there since 1932 and still hold on. Theirs is a first-class story, meatier than *Robinson Crusoe* and *The Swiss Family Robinson* combined, but we can't stop to tell it here. We have our own return to the Galápagos to deal with.

Our years on Floreana proved to us that—given luck, which we had—life was possible in the Enchanted Islands even on the terms we had contracted for it—quite impossible, unthinkable terms in the estimation of most people. But we could not forget Santiago, where the terms were, if conceivable, even worse. The trouble was that we had not been allowed to stay there long enough and the mystery of it kept on calling. Perhaps we are like recalcitrant children—deny us something and we want it twice as much. And perhaps—must I confess it?—we were just a little touched by the Dream of Avalon, of Paradise, of the Happy Hunting Grounds. You know, that mirage which flickers on the inside of your eyelids when you close them and say the words "desert island." In an endless expanse of blue sea a little green spot with a couple of coco-nut trees on it. You under the coco-nuts. Peace and *dolce far niente* and *laissez faire* all around. Ecce Paradise!

However, only just touched—but most barely. Santiago is not like that—not to the biggest idiot, if he has seen it. We had.

Five years and more in the Galápagos should have been enough for anybody who had not hanged Moros at seventeen or cut her milk teeth on blood pancakes, but we have done those things and their mark will be on us as long as we live. Only a long train of the grimmer circumstances can take you to a place that is known as the world's end, as almost any Galápagan can tell you.

Ainslie was dragged by a train like this:

At seventeen he finished high school and joined the army. He should have been eighteen and he really had meant to join the navy—and see the world, of course. But when he walked out of the Ferry Building in San Francisco, with only the useless

SANTIAGO ISLAND

stub of a railroad ticket in his pocket, the first thing he came
to was an army recruiting office. The city was strange and con-
fusing, the boy was lonely, the recruiting officer was friendly,
and the army pay, in addition to room and board, was fifteen
dollars a month. Lately there had been shooting trouble with
the Moros in the Philippines, and the officer told Ainslie that he
might be sent there very soon and so get a chance to see that
world. A little cash in the boy's pocket might have kept him
from joining up, but not having it, he became forthwith a fifteen-
dollar-a-monther. With a small difference, however, from the
lowest of the low: he was a few feet from the bottom, the height
of a good horse's rump above the ground, for he was in the
cavalry.

For a California mountain boy the cavalry was a cinch. His
six feet of lank muscle and bone had grown up in the saddle
and he had shot his own rabbits since he was seven. Within six
months he had hop-skip-and-jumped from recruit to sergeant,
made a thirty-day crossing of the Pacific—seasick all the way to
Jolo—and hanged his first Moro.

The Moros are Moors and Mohammedans—*Moro* means
Moor. To them Ainslie and his young buddies, who had never
given religion a thought, were infidels and, more horrid still,
Christians. Moreover, dirty Christians who ate pork. The
Moros were good fighters, especially disconcerting with the
knife. Ainslie's first sight of a Christian guard caught napping
by a sneaking, crawling, knife-bearing Moro made him sicker
than green apples had ever done.

Some of Ainslie's duties as a Christian soldier were mind-
broadening. Once he forcibly put shoes on a Moro insurgent
who was about to be hanged. The regulations said that the
hangee must be fully and decently clothed before he was brought
to the gallows. The central character in this scene had never
worn shoes before in all his life and naturally he objected to dying
in them—especially Christian shoes. It was perhaps some comfort to the Moro that he was not to be buried in them. Ainslie
had orders to take the shoes off the corpse as soon as it stopped
kicking, and they were used to put the proper note of decency
into the next hanging.

After a three-year stretch in the Philippines, Ainslie re-
enlisted for lack of something better to do and was sent to the
Mexican border, where a bunch of bandits led by Villa were
singing "La Cucaracha." To Ainslie the most memorable event
of this campaign was herding several hundred Mexican refugees

into cattle cars and taking them to a camp near Sierra Blanca,
Texas. On the way one of the women began having a baby in
the car Ainslie was chaperoning, and the other Mexicans were
either too hysterical or apathetic to help her. Ainslie, as officer
in charge, felt responsible—Ainslie always feels responsible—and
remembering the calves he had seen delivered, he caught the
little brown squaller as he popped out, wrapped him in the
mother's shawl, and ordered a private to clean up. Giving this
order made him feel like a cavalry sergeant again.

Then came the first World War, and Ainslie found himself a
first lieutenant teaching field artillery at Fort Snelling. This was
the result of a mistake—someone higher up had confused him
with another Conway. For three months Ainslie was so busy
learning what his students knew already that he learned to live
without sleeping. Then someone who knew him came around
to inspect, and Ainslie was sent back pronto to his horse, and
a couple of months later to France.

Ainslie seems to have forgotten nearly everything about those
two years over there. He only remembers that the French
general who pinned a Croix de Guerre on him and kissed him
on both cheeks had very curly and ticklish whiskers.

In the early twenties Ainslie got out of the army—this, too,
he says, was a mistake. After that his life has been one mistake
after another—policeman, prohibition agent, miner, construction superintendent. The result is that now he can handle
almost any job and feel thoroughly out of place in it.

I met Ainslie in 1935—he mistook me for another woman, not
the second daughter in a family of seven other daughters and
three sons who had been brought up on an ordinary Minnesota
dirt farm that produced everything we had for daily food except
sugar, coffee, pepper, and salt. This meant that everybody who
could toddle worked for a living. I had daily duties of dish-
washing, floor-sweeping, pig-feeding, chicken-feeding, egg-
gathering, cow-milking, and baby-tending. The hours I spent
baby-tending could not be laid end to end—it just wouldn't be
practical. And in between these ordinary chores were extraordinary ones.

Butchering day came about six times a year. On those days
mother or big sister would hold a large dishpan under the slit
throat of a squealing pig or bawling steer as it slowly bled to
death. Then they would bring the foaming, dripping, crimson
panful into the kitchen and call peremptorily: "Fanny!" (That
name is one of my lesser crosses.) I would put the current baby

into his crib and come running. A large whisk made of peeled willow twigs would be thrust into my hand, and mother or sister would rap out: "Stir this blood until it gets cool, so it won't clot." And I would beat and stir for all my thin wrist was worth, admiring the rich red colour and dreaming of the blood pancakes and blood sausage I would eat that evening.

With my brothers I snared rabbits, trapped muskrats, flayed dead calves, killed and dressed chickens, tied up surplus kittens and puppies in gunny sacks weighted with stones and threw them into the lake, caught gophers alive by cupping my hands over the holes as the boys flushed them out with bucketfuls of water. Once while digging potatoes with a garden fork I drove the fork through my foot. I could tell you how mother treated the wound, but I won't. You couldn't take it.

I draw a merciful veil over a few other things, too, and skip to the time when I left home at thirteen to attend high school. Then I blot out a few more horrid memories, until I find myself a university graduate, a school-teacher, and—so I thought—a lady. That thought has long since gone the way of all illusions.

With all those earlier experiences fermenting in our memories, where could we go but to the Galápagos? But having once taken that cure and been graduated with honours, why take it again? In the first place we neurotics are like that, and in the second our treatment had given us another ailment.

The tropics, they say, "will get into your blood." So will desert islands. I dare say even Crusoe, who had started his career as a pirate in the Caribbean and other exotic seas, yearned now and then for his San Juan Fernandez after he was safely beached, and reformed, in England. When you have been exposed to a combination of tropics and desert islands—and when those islands are, moreover, enchanted islands—what can you expect? Everything else thereafter seems tame and pale and namby-pamby. You feel fenced in. You get claustrophobia.

And even while you know that, once you are back among the blue horizons, the far-off shores, the spellbound deserts, you will turn around and yearn with equal nostalgia for the fabulous cities, the fantastic gadgets, the heavenly comfort of the civilisation you left behind—still you pack up and go. You are now in two pieces. One part of you wants one thing, the other part wants the opposite. You are lost. And there is no help for you anywhere.

So, condemned half-chicks that we are, for ever trying to make contact with the other half, in December, 1946, we were on our way back to the Enchanted Islands—by way of Mexico City, Vera Cruz, Balboa, Quito, and Guayaquil.   Part of the way we had travelled by bus, the rest by train and air, and we were now doing the last and most rugged stretch on board the oldest warship in active service.   The situation was as bad as that.

We and our ton or so of equipment and supplies had permission from the Ecuadorian government to stay as long as we liked on Santiago.

II. THE OLDEST WARSHIP IN ACTIVE SERVICE

A LITTLE brown mess-boy in a man-size white jacket came to
announce dinner for the first sitting—the table in the messroom
seated only eight. The food was as we had expected—the usual
soup, salad, meat, beans, rice, and black coffee, served in courses
on not half enough dishes, which kept the mess-boys hopping.
Good white bread and half-melted butter were present at this
first meal, but everybody knew from experience that they would
not last out the trip. We all wondered why the butter had not
been refrigerated, since there was an electric refrigerator in that
very room. The guest who was seated nearest the refrigerator
door opened it to see. The shelves were filled with beer and
Pepsi-Cola bottles, half of them empty.

Our table companions were also as expected, though that
does not mean that they were "ordinary" people—ordinary
people are not likely to be found on Galápagos-bound vessels.
Except for the Ecuadorians themselves, who may be plain, honest
ciitzens, the passengers are either queer or distinguished.

Facing us were two old acquaintances—Carlos Gil, the
Ecuadorian *padrón* of Isabela, and Karl Kuebler, an ex-German
diplomat, naturalised citizen of Ecuador, and for a dozen years
one of the more noteworthy inhabitants of Santa Cruz. Hans
Angermeyer, also a German colonist of Santa Cruz, was accompanied by his wife, Emma, who was coming to the Galápagos
for the first time. She turned out to be a citizen of the United
States and a graduate of the University of Nebraska, my own
Alma Mater. We shook hands and said, "It's a small world."

One of the new faces intrigued me because so little of it
was in sight. It was covered with a dark, bushy growth of
foot-long whiskers. The man's neck too was covered, front and
back, for his hair reached his shoulders. Not knowing his name
nor daring to ask—I had already asked a couple of wrong questions that day—I privately nicknamed him Nature Boy. With
him was a woman who spoke the Oakie dialect and indeed was
from Oklahoma. She was middle-aged or more, some twenty
years older than her companion, who hailed, I understood, from
Michigan.

These two were also desert island seekers—they said they wanted to find a place where they could be by themselves and live according to nature. Since an island for ourselves was our quarry, too, we were not exactly pleased to find so soon two other *norte-americanos* who sought the same thing in the same place. Our new friends were not exactly pleased either and for exactly the same reason. And Ainslie, who thinks all *norte-americanos* should look like cavalry officers, was embarrassed by Nature Boy's bumper crop of hair.

We knew our way around pretty well on the *Calderón*, for this was our second voyage on her. Our first trip had been in 1937, when we were evacuated from Santiago to Floreana. Except for the loss of the awning and the gun, ten years had made very little difference in the aspect of the warship—she had reached the age when a few years one way or the other mean practically nothing. About the time of the Civil War in the United States she had been built for Italy and later worn out in her service. Italy had sold her to Chile, where she had been worn out again. In her turn Chile had sold the veteran to Ecuador, under whose flag she had been dry-docked, overhauled, repaired, reconditioned, and rebuilt heaven knows how many times.

However, since Ecuador cannot afford to discard anything as long as there is a tin can's worth of it left, and no other nation is so poor as to buy the *Calderón* except for scrap iron, the ship was still at work—and good work it was too, considering the terrific difficulties she met and overcame daily. Only Ecuadorians could successfully man a ship like her, for only they could muster the ironic patience and fatalistic courage she demanded as tribute to her unmatched age. Though perhaps patience and courage had little to do with it. Perhaps the ancient *Calderón* was so much like Ecuador herself, so much like the Ecuadorian people, who are also durable and mongrel of origin and whose lives are a patchwork of custom and improvisation, that the enfeebled ship and her querulous, old-woman's demands seemed only natural to her commanders and crews.

When the little *comandante* had us to dinner at the officers' mess one day—this is a customary courtesy extended to all first-class passengers on each voyage—he related a much-repeated anecdote in a manner lightly touched with irony and heavily underlined with pride.

During the late war, when the *comandante* was in the Canal Zone—having his ship repaired there, for that too is customary

—the commander of a Mexican destroyer, which also happened to be in the Zone and no doubt for the same purpose, invited the Ecuadorian abroad his vessel.

"The drinks are on me," said the Mexican, "for I have the honour to command the oldest warship in active service."

"Really?" said the Ecuadorian, keen to guard his honour. "How old is your vessel?"

"Not a year less than seventy."

"Ah, my friend," returned the Ecuadorian—no doubt expanding his chest and twirling his moustache—"with your permission, the drinks are on me. *Señor Comandante*, I command the oldest warship in active service. The *Calderón* is eighty-five years old."

Under cover of the ensuing laughter, the *comandante* stabled his upper plate and then pointed to an elaborate scroll which covered a large part of the wall to his right.

"That will prove to you that the *Calderón* is still a battle-worthy ship in spite of her age and present peaceful and menial pursuits," he said, pointing. "That scroll commemorates the heroism of the officers and crew of my ship in the glorious battle of Jambelí."

We all looked and admired, then turned to the *comandante* expecting him to tell us the details of that battle, but he said no more. Though we had heard those details many times before, we were a little disappointed, for the *comandante*'s version of them would have been enlightening."

About 1940, during the war between Ecuador and Peru, the *Calderón* was on patrol duty somewhere off the coast near Jambelí, Peru. One day the look-out saw something that might have been an enemy submarine, or a whale, or a porpoise. Adither with excitement, the Ecuadorian commander had the *Calderón*'s one ancient three-incher brought to bear on the enemy.

The gun was fired—for the first time in twenty years.

Action was indeed glorious. There was a tremendous boom and the crash and scream of splintering wood. For a few moments everyone was too shocked to realise what had happened. But soon enough was told a sad story. The gun was gone. Half the deck was gone. Two seamen were gone. And, indeed, the enemy was gone.

The *Calderón* crawled back to Guayaquil—fortunately and miraculously the engine was still in working order—and from there to the Canal Zone for repairs. The deck was replaced, as were the two seamen; but with the expenses of the war and all, the national treasury was too badly depleted to afford a new gun. In its place the government ordered a bronze plaque to be attached to the spot where the gun had been—this was much cheaper—and the scroll engraved and put up where it would do the most good. It would be salutary and encouraging for future generations of the *Calderón's* officers to remember the glorious action at Jambelí.

"It takes heroes to fight a war with a ship like the *Calderón*," I said seriously.

The *comandante* smiled. "We like to think so," he said. "Though, frankly, as a naval officer I don't like it. The peace-time service she performs now is much more important than anything she has ever done in war. But—it lacks dignity." He glanced wistfully at the scroll, where his own name did not appear. Another man had had the good fortune to be in command at Jambelí.

With a feeling of guilt I thought of the iron roofing, the empty oil drums, the many sacks and packing boxes filled with beans, rice, tools, and other odds and ends which comprised our share of the unwarlike freight the *Calderón* was then carrying in her hold and in every other nook and corner, though our share was very small compared with the total. And we meant to add to it the disgrace of a couple of donkeys and a half-dozen chickens at San Cristóbal Island, our first port in the Galápagos.

At that time, the *Calderón* was the only vessel, warlike or peacelike, which made regular—well, somewhat regular—trips between continental Ecuador and her famous island possessions. Since several of the islands are garrisoned and colonised, the *Calderón's* services in that region were as essential to the functioning of island economy as are the services of the optic nerve to the functioning of the eye. Certainly her services were now necessary to the functioning of the Conways. We had waited two months in Guayaquil for the *Calderón* to make her present trip, and, if she had not been on the job, we might have waited two years.

Ecuador has at least two other warships newer and better than the *Calderón*. A destroyer or two acquired in a deal with the United States have diesel motors—and diesel engineers are rare in Ecuador. Also it is not dignified to use the newer ships for donkey's work, except when the *Calderón* is in dry dock. Another ship, once a Vanderbilt yacht, but reconditioned as a warship, remains at anchor in the Guayas Estuary. It costs more than fifty dollars just to move her to a new anchorage—obviously the price of the Galápagos circuit for her would empty the national treasury. Moreover, she too is equipped with diesel engines. The *Calderón, gracios a Dios,* works with steam.

She works with dark, viscous crude oil too, as we discovered on the first night out. Like all first-class passengers on this Jill-of-all-trades, we had been given "Helen Gould" cots to set up on deck or in the dining-cabin below. Together with a half-dozen other hardened individuals, we preferred the deck. The three other women and their husbands crowded their cots into the cabin, first taking apart the extension table and pushing the pieces against the wall. The night was chilly, they had with them only thin cotton blankets, and the *Calderón* furnished no bedding. Bitter experience had taught us something about voyaging on Ecuadorian ships, and we had brought our mattresses and heavy woollen blankets so rolled up that they could be spread out in one easy movement. We meant to be comfortable, though most of the other travellers considered the mattresses ostentatious. Each set of circumstances has its own conventions, and in our present element being properly equipped was not correct.

There was nothing between us and the stars except a few shreds of wind-blown clouds. Rain was scarcely probable at that season, yet at midnight we were awakened by something like rain in our faces. There was an excited movement among our bed-fellows and the cry, "*Aceite, aceite!*" There was an excited movement among the Conways too as we piled out to drag our cots away from the spray of crude oil blowing out of a leaking pipe. Our faces and bedding were already sticky with it, as were the deck and everything on it. "What a time this would be for a fire!" I thought. I always think of those things.

I also thought of the second-class passengers on the forward deck—twice as many of them in half as much space as served us fortunate ones. Men, women and children, they were huddled body to body under thin blankets on the bare boards. I envied them. They were not sprayed with crude oil.

The engineering department got busy with a rapidity that indicated experience. The leakage was stopped, for the time. We had only just settled back in bed when the faulty whistle sprayed us with a fine drizzle of condensed steam. This lasted only a few minutes, for the engineers did their duty again, speedily and without excitement. And we slept for a while.

Before the night was over we woke with a feeling that something was not as it had been until then. We were right.

The engines had stopped. Our fellow passengers sat up with appropriate words—"*Quée pasa?*" and "*Dios mío!*" were the quotable phrases. A stout old *cholo* was the first to lie down again. "*Caramba pues,*" he said, "if the engines stop is that a reason for me to stop sleeping?" And he pulled his blanket over his face.

"Sensible old so-and-so," said Ainslie, and we too lay back on our pillows. But, no matter what, we kept ourselves awake for an hour waiting for the engines to move. They did not move and we forgot to wait.

It was barely dawn when we were awake again, and so were the others. Something was happening. Yes, the engines were turning over. Oh well, in another twenty-four hours, we would be as imperturbed as the *Calderón*'s own crew, and nothing short of honest-to-god disaster could excite us.

As the sun climbed up, hot and bright and inescapable, the *Calderón* moved into rougher water. The green seas slopped over on the lower deck and flooded the floor of the dining-cabin, where the first-class hand luggage was piled on the floor along the walls. The passengers who preferred to stay below salvaged the bags, including ours, and we let them do it. We were not going into that airless box that day. It was enough exertion to reel into the washroom and the toilet the minimum number of times—though these were popular places.

We tried to stay on our feet, for in that position we absorbed less sunlight. We also tried to recapture the mood of our first trip to the Galápagos on the well-remembered *San Cristóbal* ten years ago. And we tried to find pleasure in the foam-flecked blue sea, the clean blue sky, and the sporting dolphins. Our failure in the first of these objectives prevented the success of the others.

So we lay on our cots in the full glare of the sun, our wide monte-cristi hats over our faces. By noon I was soaking in perspiration, but I dared not take off my jacket for fear of burning my arms. Ainslie fell asleep and, in turning over, pulled up the legs of his trousers. Around mid-afternoon he woke to a burning pain, and the next day both his legs wore blisters, like inflated toy balloons, six inches across.

Even so, our troubles were just a little more pepper in the pepper sauce, or the other half of the price of travelling on the world's oldest warship—the money half of the price was ridiculously small considering the high privilege it bought. And we had not boarded the *Calderón* expecting a ride on the *Queen Mary*.

Our seasickness left us at nightfall, but by way of keeping our fingers crossed we did not eat any dinner, though we had missed lunch too. We had another midnight awakening, and my trouble this time was a ravenous stomach. I dug into a little handbag I had under my cot and brought out a handful of stale Guayaquil crackers and a jar of olives. Ainslie did as the other men were in the habit of doing at the rail of the darkened ship at midnight and then smoked a cigarette. He turned down my offer of refreshments, but as he listened to me crunching the crackers, he changed his mind and ate two olives. "I wish they were ham sandwiches," he said.

"In Ecuador one keeps on wishing for ham sandwiches," I reminded him.

In the morning we went down to breakfast—our ration was two crackers, one boiled egg, and one cup of black coffee with sugar. I let Ainslie have my egg—it was a one-minute egg, and blood-eater though I am, I cannot eat eggs quite that raw.

We found the ship's doctor on the deck reading Emil Ludwig. He complained of idleness and boredom and said that he had to read in order to pass time.

"You are the very man I want to see then," Ainslie said. "The blisters on my legs should help speed up a few minutes."

Immediately the doctor was all bustle and concern. He took Ainslie to his little dispensary, where an enlisted assistant was also passing time, though without the help of Mr. Ludwig. The doctor glanced at the burns, spoke briefly to the assistant, assured Ainslie that with the treatment he had prescribed the burns would be quite healed up the next day, and went back on deck to pass time. The assistant broke the blisters, slapped on something sticky and yellow, followed up with bandage, and, in his turn, soothed the patient with the promise that all would be well the next day.

On the fourth day out, when we were approaching San Cristóbal Island, Ainslie's legs felt much worse, and peeking under the bandages he found signs of infection. He looked for the doctor and was told that *el medico* was in his state-room resting. Ainslie found the assistant in the dispensary and bribed him to dress the burns again, without the doctor's directions. This time the medication was some sort of powder, probably antiseptic.

III. SO HERE WE ARE AGAIN

On entering Wreck Bay, the *Calderón* passed so close by a ruined castle of an islet that the passengers gathered at the rail to see just how close she would get. They were not quite trusting those whimsical engines. But enveloped in a long over-coat and rigid and correct on the bridge, the little *comandante* knew where he had to go. Across the bay stretched a long reef and upon it the rollers were rumbling and foaming. The tide was low. At high tide the reef was quite invisible, and more than one vessel had dashed her bottom out while trying a short cut into the harbour. The sunken hulks of those unfortunates had given the bay its name. Otherwise it was a lovely piece of water, blue and shimmering, and edged with black lava and white surf. The ship dropped her anchor a quarter-mile from the beach which is the waterfront of the capital of the Galápagos.

Puerto Chico, known to her officials as Puerto de Baquerizo Moreno, is a typical Ecuadorian village—or as typical as it can be in the Encantadas. It is built of bamboo, corrugated iron, native matasarno wood, and whatever else is handy. Behind a good beach of yellow-white sand it lies on a limestone flat hemmed in by ancient, brush-covered lava flows. The Oakie woman who was our fellow passenger liked it at first sight. She said it was "real pretty."

Many of the two-hundred or so inhabitants are former "exiled" prisoners, now free colonists, or their descendants. They live by fishing, trading, politics, and taking in each other's washing. Racially they are a fairly rich mixture of Nordic white, Mediterranean white, and Quechua Indian.

I noticed several new buildings that had not been there on our first visit to the place. Puerto Chico had not escaped pro-gress. A red-roofed barracks, a hospital, a schoolhouse, and a picturesque "commissary" of red-painted lumber and dark-grey lava now faced the ocean. Our friends on board were quick to inform us that the hospital had no equipment and the commissary had no provisions, but the buildings gave dignity to the place, anyway. The school did have pupils—some thirty dark-faced children were enjoying "recess" on the beach in front of the building. Presently we heard the clanging of the school bell, a piece of iron pipe struck with a piece of the same, and the children moved toward the building with a crablike gait—their feet were pointed schoolward but their heads were turned seaward where the ship had just dropped anchor.

Another thing was new and it reminded us of recent world events: a grey army tug and an immense water-barge were tied to the old wharf. During the war Uncle Sam had constructed a ten-mile pipeline from a lake near the centre of the island to the beach and a couple of storage reservoirs. Baltra Island, where Uncle had his Galápagos airbase, is a waterless waste of lava and tufa dust, and the tug and barge brought fresh water from Puerto Chico to Baltra, making the trip, one way, in about eight hours.

Though the officers courteously let us go ashore in the first boat, which is usually reserved for the nation's anointed, we were not board-hopping the old matasarno wharf until four o'clock, and the word was that the *Calderón* would pull out at seven in the morning. Even on good legs the ten-mile trip to the plantations inland could not be made that evening, and Ainslie was scarcely able to limp about in the deep sand of the beach. We tried to send natives to get us the animals, fruit, and vegetables we wanted to buy, but found none willing to leave the beach while two ships were at anchor in the bay. Our business would have to be done at Puerto Chico or not at all.

After bargaining and conferring until nightfall, chiefly with women whose minds were on other business, we bought three donkeys, four chickens, and one dog, and received the promise that they would be put aboard the ship before seven in the morning.

A tiny barefoot *chola*, wearing a wide-skirted blue dress, and two long braids of hair, sold me fifty pounds of small red potatoes and the same weight of over-age but under-size *camotes* (sweet potatoes). "Lovely *camotes*," she gushed to the fool-*gringo*, who, of course, did not know any better. She had the grace to explain that she had sold her really choice products to the army tug earlier in the day, though not enough grace to lower her prices. "The *gringos* on the tug pay like crazy," she confided artlessly, as she dug into the bosom of her dress and brought out a roll of bills. The top bill was ten dollars, United States' style. She covered it with my twenty *sucres*, Ecuadorian style, and tucked the roll back into the "safe."

As I glanced around the bare, bamboo-walled room that

served her as shop and living quarters to see if she might have something else for sale, she said: "Sell me some soap, *señora*. I'm all out."

"What about that soap?" I asked, pointing to some six bars of Palm Olive on a dusty shelf.

"Oh, that is for sale. I can't afford to use it myself. Imported soap is too expensive. I want national soap."

"I'm sorry," I said, "but I have enough soap only for our own use. We'll need it all on Santiago."

"So you are going to Santiago? I have a boy, sixteen years old, well brought up and a good worker. Take him with you. We are going to build a new house, and his wages would help us."

"But we can't take him. We have supplies only for ourselves. And the boy would be too lonely on Santiago."

"*Dios mío*, then, *señora*, sell me some sugar. The men from the ship say you have four *quintales*."

"We are going to need it all."

"Out of four hundred pounds you can surely sell ten pounds," she insisted.

"But it is deep in the hold with tons of other stuff piled on top of it. Don't you make *raspadura* (home-made brown sugar) out of your cane juice any more?" I knew that the woman's husband cultivated several acres of sugar-cane in the uplands.

The *chola* covered her face with her hand, as if in mock shame.

"No, we all make nothing but *puro* (rum) now. It is easier and brings more money."

Before she could think of any more business, I extended my hand to say good-bye. Instead of her grubby fingers she offered me her wrist, which I touched ceremoniously. "My hand is dirty," she said.

Near the beach a Quechua woman in the characteristic red shawl and black felt hat was sitting on the ground under an *algarobo* tree. Beside her stood an exhausted old donkey and two old kerosene tins containing roast pork and boiled corn on the cob. It was past supper-time and we were hungry. Each of us bought a half-pound of pork and two ears of corn, which we ate on the spot from our hands.

Herr Kuebler, who had come ashore to take a fresh-water bath under one of Uncle Sam's water faucets on the beach, saw us eating and came to get his own supper, too. He gave me a recipe for cooking sea iguana—his own invention—and I made careful note of it, thinking I might need it.

I asked the Quechua woman if we could get any bananas, pine-apples, or any fruit at all.

"I have a few oranges," she answered glumly, and went to her saddle-bags to get them. "Many people brought burro-loads of fruit and vegetables down from their *chacras* today, but they soon sold them all. The *gringos* bought everything."

Our hard luck. We consoled ourselves by eating six oranges apiece.

Next morning the animals were not on board at seven, nor

yet at eight, and the commander made important business of telling Ainslie to hurry. Ainslie hobbled ashore again, deter-mined to fire the breeches of his agents, and at nine we no longer bore the blame for delay. The donkeys were half-dead from their swim in sea water and crude oil—the *Calderón* was leaking oil again—but they were soon rubbed down and on their feet. Hans Angermeyer was looking for a bucket to give them water, and Herr Kuebler was soothing them with potatoes, *camotes,* pats, clucks, and baby-talk. Wherever there are Germans, animals are well cared for. Later Kerr Kuebler came to tell me that the donkeys had kissed him by way of thanks. "Animals as well as people show their affection with the mouth," he said.

When Herr Kuebler saw the bitch pup, he immediately went

to stroke her and offer water and sweet words. In a dither of delight the dog licked his hands and face, and Herr Kuebler was in his turn so delighted that he offered to buy the dog for twice as much as we had paid for her. "She likes me," he gushed, "and I love dogs better than human beings. I have often been betrayed by men, never by dogs." We were sure that the dog would be happier with Kuebler than with us, but for even four times her cost we could not sell her to him.

At ten o'clock the *Calderón* was still taking in water and leaking out oil. The cook went ashore to buy fresh meat and came back with a large live hog. I asked him how much he had paid for his find and he answered: "Two hundred *sucres*"— which then amounted to something like eleven dollars.

Twelve o'clock, and we were finally on our way to Baltra Island. The whistle tooted, the dog howled, the donkeys brayed, and the pig squealed. When things had quieted down, the rooster had the last word.

At the air base the next morning Ainslie went ashore to buy cigarettes at the post exchange—he wanted at least ten cartons. In the evening he came back, lame and exhausted, with one package of Chesterfields and five ounces of pipe tobacco. All the Ecuadorians on the ship had gone ashore and all had wanted to buy cigarettes, which meant that they had to be rationed.

Business was good in the Galápagos.

CACTI AND LAVA

CONWAY'S WATER HOLE

IV. GLOOM UNDER A LOW SKY

For several hours before the *Calderón* anchored in James Bay, we had been skirting the south shore of Santiago, much the worst side for a prospective settler to look on first. We had seen it before, of course, but only dimly, in misty moonlight, and all we had been able to make out was an immense, dark, many-humped mass floating in a grey sea. Now the details were clear.

The contour went up and down irregularly, like a cosmic coal heap carelessly thrown together. And I thought of coal with good reason, for at least fifty square miles of the visible area was raw, black lava and no vegetation of any kind was evident on it. The remaining surface was covered with scrubby trees and shrubbery, now mostly grey and leafless or only slightly touched with dusty green. On the shore, here and there, were clumps of brilliant green mangrove set off by little white coral beaches and black lava cliffs and plateau. The surf was white all along the line. A low, cloudy sky added gloom to the picture.

At James Bay the view was more reassuring—the green highlands were coming into sight as a thick mist cleared away. The tawny-grey tufa cliffs, the extinct crater of Sugar Loaf, and the great lava flow were as we remembered them, but the nearer lowlands were dry and grey, as if a thick coat of dust had settled on them in our absence.

On the little landings the surf was rather rough, and Ainslie was already worried about the sugar and flour that might get dunked in the sea before they reached dry land. I was just worried.

No one else seemed worried. The officers had been drinking beer all morning—after a night at the air base they needed a few hairs of the old dog—it was lunch-time, and a spirit of holiday had taken possession of the crew. No one seemed to care when the Conways got ashore, if at all.

We waited. I ate some lunch—a plateful of fresh pork chops and fried corn which I could not ignore—but Ainslie fidgeted and jittered. He prowled along the deck, three paces in one direction, three in the other—that was all the room there was.

Finally a boat was lowered. Neither we nor any of our goods

went into it. Several officers, with Herr Kuebler and Nature Boy, were going ashore to hunt goats.

On the beach the boat crew ran around for an hour trying to catch a seal which fortunately escaped to sea, after which they all went swimming. Eventually and reluctantly they returned to the ship, and after another delay Conway got off with one boatload of his stuff. He directed the boat to be landed on a little beach sheltered by the western arm of the bay, where the surf was less active. I watched the overloaded boat anxiously, expecting trouble, but it made the landing in good shape.

The men took out another boatload successfully—this time the dog was taken along and Hans Angermeyer went with her to comfort her, for she was terrified of the rough-handed sailors. Another unfortunate seal came flopping confidently on the rocks, and the chase this time was aided by the dog. The chasers were drenched with sea water, but the seal was caught. Evidently the law which was supposed to protect him did not reach as far as the Galápagos. The sailors took time to skin the seal before they brought the boat back.

Meantime we had heard four shots from the direction where the hunters and the explorer had gone. Now they came back to the middle beach, which is at the right of the lava flow—our name for it is the Goya Rico beach—and they were carrying two goats. They signalled for the boat and got it. All but Herr Kuebler came aboard. The energetic Kuebler had gone after another goat.

One more boatload went out for Conway at his beach. I stood on the well-deck checking off the items on a typewritten lists we had prepared in Guayaquil. A young ensign stood beside me to see that everything was correct and official. Ainslie had remained ashore to handle things at that end. Now Herr Kuebler had returned and was sporting on the sand, gutting and washing a goat and taking a refreshing swim in the sea. Presently he signalled for the boat—which took off to fetch him.

Eventually two more boatloads went out for us, and I was getting ready to take myself off with the last load, when the *comandante* sent me an order to wait and directed the boatmen to tell Ainslie to come back aboard. Ainslie came—his shoes full of sand and his face full of weariness.

"What does the *comandante* want now?" he asked me. I could not tell him.

A sailor directed us to the officers' messroom, where we found the commander seated at the head of the table, his face flushed and his eyes bleary. Near him sat the black-bearded young executive officer, holding in his hand a long typewritten sheet of many columns.

The commander invited us to be seated—he did not rise as a *gringo* officer nearly always does in the presence of a woman no matter how sun-burned and frazzled—and told the bearded one to speak his piece.

"You owe the Ecuadorian government nine hundred and ninety-nine *sucres* for the transportation of your goods," said the executive officer. "I have the itemised list here in my hands."

Neither Ainslie nor I could think of anything to say for fully two minutes—minutes which the officers filled in by putting their heads together and studying the list.

"But why?" Ainslie asked finally. "At the naval office in Guayaquil we were told that we could bring in free everything we needed for our personal use. We brought nothing to sell."

"But it is always customary to pay," said the commander, getting a little excited—evidently he had not expected an argument. "No ship in the world carries freight for nothing."

"Then why did the Guayaquil office tell us that there would be no charge?" I asked.

The commander shrugged. "They probably meant only your hand luggage. You brought much more than that."

"But I asked the official particularly just how much we could bring," Ainslie insisted, "and he said we could bring all we needed."

"Did you read your ticket?" the bearded one asked. "Here is a copy of it. Read what it says and inform yourself." His tone was not polite.

I could feel my face growing pale, for we had not read everything printed on the ticket—we had not even thought of looking on the back of it. Could it be that we really owed a thousand *sucres* to Ecuador? Dreadful thought—for we had scarcely that much left, and I, for one, was determined not to part with much of it—certainly not the five hundred I had pinned to my underwear. I was sure the *comandante* would not order one of his underlings to search me—though on second thought I was not so sure. I remembered the incident of the sword.

We read the back of the ticket and began to feel better. Good old Ecuador! The Ecuadorian government asked only the payment of five *sucres* for each hundredweight over a *prudential* amount. We felt that we had less than a sane person would consider prudential for an indefinite stay on an uninhabited island like Santiago, and we told the commander so.

"Oh no, you have more!" contradicted the *comandante*, but in more words. In fact, he made a ten-minute speech, which was lengthened to fifteen minutes by interpolations and additions of "You are perfectly right, *mi comandante*," "That is quite true, *mi comandante*," "Anybody can see that, *mi comandante*," and other such yes-yessing phrases from the bearded one. "The ticket means that two or three hundredweight is a prudential amount. And you have a list here two pages long."

"But the ticket does not specify two or three quintals," I finally had the chance to say. "It specifies no amount whatever. And who is to say what prudential means? It would mean different things in different situations." I was being strictly logical, and that did not improve the commander's temper.

There were words, streams of them, from both officers, but we were too tired to count or listen. When there was a moment of silence, Ainslie turned logical. "All right," he said. "Suppose we agree that two or three hundredweight of provisions and equipment is prudential—that only so much is necessary for two people who are to live alone indefinitely on a desert island. Or suppose we forget all about prudence. How many quintals of stuff do you think we have altogether, *comandante*? No one has weighed it, of course, but what would be your estimate?"

The commander consulted the list and conferred with his assistant. He touched his moustache and considered. "About forty or fifty quintals," he said.

We did not have that much—probably only thirty quintals—but we let the estimate pass. "So then," I said, "forty quintals at five *sucres* each, would make two hundred *sucres*. How do you arrive at the figure nine hundred and ninety-nine?"

The *comandante* did not answer, but looked at me as if surprised. He was probably not used to women who figured and was caught short when he saw that I was such a whiz at arithmetic. I was beginning to think that the Conways had won the argument, but I did not wait long to be put back in my place. The *comandante* turned to his companion and said: "You tell them."

"The amount may come to two hundred *sucres* by weight," that one explained importantly, "but item by item it comes to more, much more. See the length of this list. There are scarce and valuable items on it—metal roofing, for instance, which can hardly be found at all in Guayaquil nowadays. And all these

tools—axe, hatchets, machete, two picks, shovels, a rake, and
many more I need not take time to name to you. And you
have as much as four quintals of rice and four of sugar. Most
people bring only one quintal of each when they come to the
Galápagos, and many bring less. Why, it took me two hours
to type a copy of this list. How can you say that you should
pay only two hundred *sucres* for the transportation of this *mundo
de cosas*?"

"Yes," said the *comandante*, "the list is extraordinarily long.
And what is more, I have given you the assistance of my officers
and men in handling your things and my boatmen have taken
them ashore. I insist that you pay me nine hundred and ninety-
nine *sucres*."

We were reminded of a fact we could not forget, anyway.
Our things were on shore, and we were on the *Calderón*—and
for how long? Night was imminent, we had camp to make,
Ainslie's burns to dress, and the boatmen were waiting. The
comandante could keep us from landing if he wanted to. He
might threaten to take us back to Guayaquil and leave our stuff
lying on the beach. Logic was of no help, for these boys did
not like logic—they had lost their tempers every time we offered
it. Would I have to excuse myself, dig out those five hundred
sucres from my brassière, and hand them over? "Over my dead
body," I thought, but that was not a comforting thought either.
The sword, I remembered, the sword. A sword is so separating,
and it could separate me from my cherished five hundred *sucres*.

Then help came from an unexpected source. From my own
head. An idea popped up. We could beat the *comandante* to
threats, if those were to be the chosen weapons. I spoke to
Ainslie in English, which the *comandante* did not understand
but the executive officer understood after a fashion. This was
my idea of the psychological approach. "Since we just don't
have that much money with us, I guess after all we must return
to Guayaquil. We could leave our things here—or take them
back and let the commander of the naval district settle the
argument about the meaning of prudential."

"What are they saying?" the *comandante* asked his assistant,
and the assistant answered: "They say they have not sufficient
money and are going back to Guayaquil."

The commander said nothing while he sucked up his upper
plate. Then he shouted: "I cannot take you back to Guayaquil.
You have tickets only to Santiago. I am authorised to take you
there, but I have no authority to take you back."

So.   Another impassable road.   But Ainslie is an experienced road maker, and he now got hold of his fly-away nerves, and came valiantly to my assistance.   He brought out cigarettes, passed them around, and lighted them.   "All we can do is to go back to Guayaquil," he said as calmly as he could.   "We can settle about permits when we get there.   Comandante Nieto, of the Guayas District, is a friend of ours, and I think I can persuade him to forgive you for taking us back without formal authorisation.   He is your superior, isn't he?

We finished our cigarettes in heavy silence.   Remembering that the *comandante* was neither quite sane nor quite sober gave us little comfort.   But the moment of silent thought helped.

Without speaking, Ainslie put two hundred-*sucre* bills on the table.   Not knowing exactly why, I laid another hundred *sucres* on top of them.

There was no protest from the *comandante*.   He pocketed the money.

"Okay," he said, using up all his English.   "Won't you stay on board for supper?   It is getting late."

We wanted to stay, if only to indicate that we were all friends again, but camp and hospital details waited.

When the boatmen were about to push off, with both of us in the boat at last, Herr Kuebler threw me a small gunny sack containing some two dozen oranges he had managed to root up at Puerto Chico.   "For the burros," he specified, "and don't forget to give them water as soon as you are ashore.   Take good care of the dog."

V. WHAT, NO COCO-NUTS?

WE were in a dry sandstone gully, scattered with a few rocks, a few scrubby bushes, a couple of dusty *muyuyu* trees, and much dead brush. During the afternoon Ainslie had piled up our equipment in a neat military manner, tethered the animals, and gathered firewood. He said that the boatmen had done an excellent job—nothing had been pilfered, nothing broken, nothing dipped in the sea.

The bandages on Ainslie's legs were black-dirty and stuck to the skin, and the burns had been increasingly painful all day. I had to play doctor and immediately. I cut off as much of the bandage as I could and soaked the rest off with peroxide. Pieces of skin came off with the gauze and left large, angry-looking splotches. There was some pus on both legs, and I washed it off with peroxide.

"I'll soak my legs in sea water tomorrow—perhaps that won't hurt quite so much," Ainslie said as he sucked in his breath and ground his teeth.

"*Paciencia*," I counselled. "The keener the pain now, the better you will feel when I am through." I was not feeling quite so high-ho as I sounded, but it seemed better to say something like that. The legs looked pretty bad to me.

When the burned areas were as clean as I dared to make them, I gave them a thick coating of antiseptic powder, applied cotton and plenty of gauze. The job was passable.

"Whew!" sighed Ainslie. "Now let's make some coffee."

Ainslie opened what we called our "landing box." In Guayaquil we had packed in it everything we thought we would need for our first "emergency" meal ashore—roasted and ground coffee, sugar, salt, jam, crackers, flour, cooking oil, baking powder, sweet chocolate, powdered milk, and sardines, as well as matches, soap, towels, and a few dishes and cooking utensils. We had brought water from Puerto Chico, very, very fortunately, in three five-gallon milk cans—and what a time we had had finding those cans in Guayaquil! Considering the parched look of the place, we were not sure there was water on Santiago now, except, perhaps, in the mountains.

You may wonder why we had not brought something more appetising for our first meal, like bacon, canned fruit, and butter. Well, for the very good reason that such delicacies are always rare in Guayaquil, and in that post-war year they were all but unobtainable in the ordinary places of sale.

We ate sardines, crackers, and coffee by firelight, for night had dropped down suddenly as it does on the equator and there was no moon. "There are fresh pork chops on the *Calderón* tonight, and perhaps *fritadas* and *chicharrones,*" Ainslie said. "And now I realise that I had no lunch."

"But lunch was served," I gave him as womanly comfort, "and supper was offered."

"So they were, but at those times my stomach juices were burning holes in their mother tissues. Another day like this and I'd have six full-blown ulcers."

"And you would have enough peace on Santiago in the next six months to heal them all. Maybe."

"And fresh goat meat tomorrow."

So there we were already, after only an hour on the island, thinking and talking of food—and thinking even more of water, though we did not say the word. In our situation, water was a sacred and potent word, not to be spoken lightly.

Ainslie put a couple of heavy *aromo* sticks on the fire to hold it until morning—there are few things so comforting as a fire or even a few glowing coals when you get up in the dank, grey dawn of a desert island. After putting away the food and dishes, we went to wash our feet in a black tide-pool in the black lava. The red port light of the *Calderón* glowed dimly on a black sea. The light looked lonelier than we felt.

Now there was nothing left to do but spread out our beds, and we were glad enough of that. Before I fell asleep I had time to reflect that I had heard no voices of the native inhabitants all afternoon—no goat-bleats, no donkey-brays, no bird-calls. I listened then for donkeys—they often bray at night—and heard nothing but our own three she-asses browsing on *muyuyu* leaves. "Did you hear any burros braying this afternoon—wild ones, I mean?" I asked Ainslie.

"Not a one—and I have been wondering about that. But I did hear mocking-birds singing."

I took comfort in the mocking-birds and was asleep presently. Around midnight I awoke with an acute feeling of being lost —a sensation of numbed helplessness. Something of the same panic must come to a sleepwalker when he wakes and finds himself two inches from the slippery edge of a railless balcony fifty feet above the ground.

"Now we have done it," I thought. "This is really the end to end all ends. Here we are, all by ourselves in this desolate, thirsty place until——" I did not know what to put after "until." It could be until anything. How could we ever get off the island? How long would we care to stay—or have to stay? We could, given water and luck, live on Santiago indefinitely, but how long is indefinitely? It could be as long as for ever.

"There are several ways we could eventually get off," I comforted myself. "We were evacuated the first time we tried Santiago—that could happen again. The officers of the *Calderón* said they would probably return to Santiago sometime. And then there is the air base on Baltra—the commanding officer there told Ainslie that he would send a plane in a few weeks to see how we were doing. Also there could be—but who knows when—a yacht, or perhaps tuna fishermen." I became so interested in these possibilities that I forgot my feeling of nightmare and fell asleep again.

Our faces, hair, and blankets were slightly wet in the morning —we had not wakened to protect ourselves from the fine predawn drizzle, after all—but the day was breaking clear and bright. The *Calderón* was pulling out, and that helped brighten up the morning too.

Ainslie said that his night-time pre-occupation had not been about "How do we get out of here, if and when?" nor about missing wild burros. "Or, rather," he said, "I did worry about the lack of donkey signs, but only because their absence indicates drought. If the springs at the foot of Sugar Loaf are running, there should be burros on the *playa*. The question now is— and it is a big, bad question—where do we get water?"

Ainslie was so anxious to hike the mile to the nearest known spring—we called it the Goya Rico spring—that he could not wait for fresh coffee. He swallowed the two cupfuls left over from last night, untied the donkeys, and limped up the side of the canyon and toward Sugar Loaf, followed by the burros and the dog.

I put a kettle of water on the fire for fresh coffee, and then rolled up the beds. When the coffee was cooked, I mixed a Dutch-oven load of biscuits which I baked in the coals and ashes of the fireplace. My breakfast was one orange, two cups of coffee, and three biscuits—they were large biscuits and good too, for my education in camp cooking is exceptionally thorough.

With all that in me, I felt so stimulated that I abandoned my housework and went exploring.

"An island of sticks and stones"—I was already talking to myself, though not out loud yet. I went up the gully—or should I call it a canyon?—ducked under the branches of the nearest *muyuyus*, and stopped there. Under the trees were two old fire-places, complete with ashes, and a crude sandstone bench. Strewn around were fish and goat bones. I found an old enamel-ware cup, a rusty knife-blade, several shards of red pottery, and something that looked like a baby's hand-crocheted cap of faded pink-and-white string. "What child could have been here?" I asked the silent air. "No child at all, silly," I answered, for the air remained silent. "Ecuadorian fishermen are likely to wear anything on their heads—from their mother's shawl to their baby's swaddling clothes. This is only a fisher-men's camp—a very old one." I gathered up my finds and put them in a box. They might be useful for something.

Beyond the *muyuyus* the canyon widened a little—it was choked with dead brush—and then divided into two canyons. A bunch of *muyuyus* stood at this division point, as well as more brush, both living and dead. To the right the canyon con-tinued—winding, stony, and brushy—but to the left it was closed up by a sandstone corral, evidently man-made.

I climbed over the low corral fence. A half-dozen *aromos* grew on the flat bottom—gnarled and twisted little trees, lightly garnished with soft, lacy leaves and bristling with two-inch thorns. Farther back was an impassable tangle of thorn-bushes —they were nothing but a mass of long, green spines. In fact, the spines served them for leaves. They were covered with small, black berries, on which a flock of doves and finches were feeding.

The corral was alive with lizards and hermit crabs. "And no doubt scorpions," I said to myself. Yes, indeed—I turned a stone in the fence and found two scorpions. Under another stone I found a centipede. And as I moved a third stone, a fourth, a fifth—a three-foot snake crawled out and slid easily under another slab of sandstone.

This menagerie might have been disconcerting if I had not already known these creatures. The scorpions would sting, if you let them, the centipedes might also be poisonous—though few people in the Galápagos pay any attention to them—but the lizards, the crabs, and the snakes were innocent and friendly. Especially the lizards were friendly—a red-throated female darted up my leg as I stood contemplating this odd sandstone bowl and its odd inhabitants and wondering who had built the place and what for.

I pushed my way through the dead brush back to my fire-place, put some more wood on the fire, and gave the chickens a little water and corn. One of them had laid an egg.

Then I climbed the side of the canyon in the direction Ainslie had taken, and came up on a sandstone-paved flat. When I say paved, I mean paved. This region was built of layers of yellowish-grey sandstone or tufa, which seemed at one time to have lain at the bottom of the sea. The tufa had cracked to form paving blocks—many of them were so neatly squared off that they looked like the work of human hands. The remains of a man-made road led off toward the Goya Rico beach just south of the lava flow. This road had probably been built by salt-gatherers who had, years ago, exploited a salt lake in a crater camp two miles from our camp. Heavy cogged wheels had left their marks in the tufa.

From where I stood, the lava and sandstone cone of Sugar Loaf seemed very close, though it was more than a mile away. The grey-white limbs of the *palo santo* trees which climbed up the dry and barren-looking slopes were bare of leaves. To the east was the flat top of the salt crater and the great, black lava flow. The forest-covered mountains beyond the lava were green at the summits, but on lower slopes most of the trees were leafless. I judged that they were *palos santos* too which always lose their leaves in the dry season—though, to be accurate, there is no really dry season in the higher altitudes of the Galápagos. On the lower slope of the nearest range an old crater, which had always been greener than any other spot in the mountains when we first knew them ten years ago, now looked peculiarly grey. "What is the matter up there?" I asked myself. "Are the trees dead?" I was specially interested in this crater, for we had once planned to make a plantation there.

"What shall we call those mountains?" I asked the wind. The wind made a thin, rustling sound in the brittle-dry weeds at my feet.

"Mountains of the Moon?" A black hawk flew over me and cried "Quee-ah, quee-ah" in a tone of raucous displeasure. "You are right," I answered him, "the moon has nothing to do with them."

"Rainbow Mountains?" I suggested a little later, as a spot of iridescence formed on a cloud of mist against the highest peak.

"Cher-níng, cher-níng!" said a tree finch, and another answered: "Quink, quink, quink, quink, quink!" The two conversed snootily, of their own business, as if naming mountains were a petty thing.

"Okay," I said, "I'll name those mountains later on when I know more about them, and not ask any of you what you think."

I turned seaward. Blue water, blue sky, white surf, black rocks. Straight north lay little Albany Island. How homelike, for some reason, to find those familiar British names attached to isolated Ecuadorian islands! Three great, violet craters of Isabela seemed to float in the sky to the west, for their bases were covered with mist. Isabela too has a fine British name, none finer—Albemarle. There are few people on Isabela and they live many unexplored miles from the mountains I could see. No one has ever lived near these craters, nor climbed them. The Ecuadorians are afraid of the volcanoes of Isabela, for some of them are still active. They are unknown land, as unknown as any land in the world these days—they and the mountains of Santiago.

The ocean was wide and empty. It seemed as if no one had ever sailed on it, nor even looked on it before. Frigate birds soared high in the lonely sky, pelicans, boobies, and gulls dived for fish. One small marine iguana scuttled along the rocks —he was exactly the colour of the lava. All these creatures were one with the scene, as impersonal and as integrated with their environment as a tree.

A tree. That reminded me. This was a "desert island"— and while it had other trees, there was not a single coco-nut palm in the place. No, not one. Leafless, white-limbed *palos santos* were scattered all over the flat with occasional dark-green *aromos* and *muyuyus*—the latter carried a few green leaves and a few yellow blossoms. The Galápagos are unique. They grow their own special kinds of trees.

There was a loud cough from the direction of Conway's Landing below me. It sounded just like a man's cough. Startled, I asked: "Who's that?" Another cough—two coughs —and then a splash. A seal poked his sleek head out of the water near the beach and flippered up on the sand. "All right," I told him, "come on up, but next time don't startle me like that."

But what was that? A glint of light, as if on glass, way off there near Albermarle Point. It could not be sunlight on the ocean—there was no such glint anywhere else on the sea, and there was an awful lot of sea. I screwed up my eyes and made a telescope of my hands. Something like a ship? Could it be the *Calderón*? No, not in that direction. Well then, a tuna fishing boat. California tuna fishermen were in the islands at this season, and one of their favourite spots was Albermarle Point.

So there I was with my spell of silence and emptiness and desert ocean and desert land. At least a dozen men were on

that tiny ship, less than five miles away—and all *gringos* too. How difficult it is to get away from people nowadays! But I had this consolation—if consolation it was—near as the tuna fishermen were, they would not come any nearer. Tuna fishermen have little time to visit—their minds are always on albacore and yellow fin and the high price of tuna in San Diego. That's what I thought, anyway.

"The fishermen are hard at work and so should you be," Conscience said. It seemed that Conscience, unbidden, had come to the islands with us. That, incidentally, is one of the difficulties of life on a desert island. Your habitual personality insists on staying right there with you.

Back among my sacks and boxes, I consulted the lists of box-contents, and unpacked the rest of the cooking utensils and such dishes and provisions as I would need the next few days.

I fetched a bucketful of sea water for washing dishes, and while I was at it, rinsed out a couple of towels in a lava-lined pool, giving dithers to the tiny purple fish swimming in it.   The seal whose coughing had startled me was asleep on the sand and I was careful not to wake him.   He, if anybody, owned the beach, though we had been arrogant enough to name it after ourselves.

For the day's heavier eating I planned to cook beans, though cooking them would use up more fresh water than I cared to think of.   Ainslie had spoken of hunting, but I was afraid he would not have the time nor the energy to kill and butcher a goat that afternoon.   He had already been gone several hours, and I wondered what was keeping him so long—it must have been something important, or hunger would have driven him back to camp before this.   Thinking of his empty stomach, I added an extra half-cupful to the beans I had measured into a washpan, and went to rinse them in the tide-pool.   Then I put the beans to soak in clean sea water.

The sun was hot, and so brilliant that it hurt my eyes.   I found my sun-glasses, went to sit on the stone bench under the shadow of the *muyuyus*—the shadow was pretty thin—and picked hulls and weed seeds out of a cupful of rice.   Presently I heard Ainslie's footsteps coming down the side of the canyon.   The dog was with him, but the donkeys were not.   His expression told me nothing except that he was tired.

"What goes?"

"Nothing too good, nothing too bad," he answered.   "Is there something to eat?"

"Of course there's something to eat.   But did you find water?"

"I did and I didn't," Ainslie said in that manner he has of building suspense.   "These biscuits are *muy buenos.*"

I asked no more questions just then.   I knew from the teasing answers that Ainslie had found conditions a trifle better than he had expected.   He finished his first cup of coffee before he went on.

"I found the spring all right, because I knew exactly where it ought to be.   But no one strange to the place could have guessed that there was water within miles of it.   The bottom of the sandstone gully where the spring breaks out was perfectly dry, and the hole Goya Rico dug in the stone bottom, ten years ago, as a little catchment basin, was filled with sand and rocks and old burro dung—in fact, the entire bottom of the gully was a foot deep in dry manure.

"I had not thought of taking the shovel and pick along with me this morning, so I worked like a fool, with my bare hands and a piece of an old iron kettle I happened to find, clearing out enough of the manure to uncover the hole. I cleaned out the stones and sand that heavy rains at some time had washed into it, and found that it was wet at the bottom. I watched for a while, and water did seep into it very slowly, and I let the dog lick it up. The whole place is so filthy that we won't get any drinking water there for several days. We'll be doing well if we get enough for the chickens and the dog."

"And the next move?" I prompted, while Ainslie lighted a cigarette.

"I'm going to take the tools up this afternoon and start cleaning out the gully—and that's a job for Hercules. To-morrow I'll carry up a piece of roofing iron to cover the hole, or the animals will smell the moisture and lick up the water as fast as it gathers. The wild donkeys are not in the habit of coming there now, and I don't want them to start coming. With them around we'll never have any clean water. There are the usual hundreds of doves and finches around the water-hole, and they alone could keep that hole dry if it is not covered up. However—things could be worse, a good deal worse, and we'll make out if the little flow we have lasts."

"In any case," he added after thinking a moment, "if the flow fails, I can rig up some sort of still out of two empty oil drums and that piece of pipe I brought and distil water from the sea. I don't like to think of that, but it is a good last resort —better than praying for rain, though even prayer may be a good idea. I'm not so sure of my influence Up There, however. How do you think you stand?"

"I can do more with spells and magic. My great-grand-father was a *brujo*."

"What about meat?" Ainslie asked when the coffee kettle was empty. "Do you think I better take the gun with me and try to get a goat? I heard some bleating not far from the spring."

"Tomorrow will do," I answered. "But did you see any wild donkeys this morning?"

"Only a couple of skeletons, and one which had evidently died a few days ago, almost on top of the spring. And I heard none. The drought must have been bad enough to kill them all—or, at least, chase them up into the mountains. Fortunately the goats seem able to live almost without water. They get enough moisture from dew or something."

"And what happened to our personal donkeys?"

"That is another thing which bothers me. I'm afraid they are goners. And what we'll do without them I don't know."

"You turned them loose then," I guessed.

"Yes. I couldn't give them any water, and running loose they may join up with wild donkeys—if there are any left—and find water somewhere on their own. I just slapped them on their rumps and said: 'Good-bye, burros. See you again, maybe, when you are too wild to do me any good.' And without pack animals I don't know how we'll ever get our stuff moved any distance, if we have to move. Right now there are a lot of things I don't know."

I was not so sure that the burros were lost—these San Cristóbal donkeys were used to living with people—but I said nothing. Better not raise any false hopes.

That afternoon when Ainslie had returned to the spring, I put my beans on to cook in a thick, aluminium Dutch oven with a tight cover, to save as much of the precious steam as possible. The soaking in sea water had already salted them so well that I could add very little salt water to the cooking liquid. And making them too salty would defeat my purpose—we could not afford to be thirsty.

My woodpile had dwindled, and while there were plenty of small sticks right around my fireplace, ready to burn after being broken over my knee in the manner my mother had taught me as a child, I needed heavier pieces for the slow fire that is best for beans. I combined work with pleasure and climbed up the side of the canyon I had not yet explored to see what I could find there. Another tufa-paved flat—part of the same flat that I had looked on in the morning though cut off from it by our camp gully—came to a point which made the western arm of James Bay and ended in a cliff at the edge of the sea. This dun-coloured *playa* was sparsely dotted with the ubiquitous *palos santos*, a few *aromos*, *muyuyus*, and even some slim *chalas*, still standing up. There had been much *chala* on the Santiago *playas* when we first knew them but now nearly all these delicate trees were lying dead on the ground. Scattered clumps of very spiny cactus, dead weeds and grass in the cracks of the sandstone, and among them multi-coloured grasshoppers and those eternal lizards.

As I looked for dry old pieces of *aromo* small enough to carry —*aromo* sticks are much too hard and tough to break over anybody's knee—I came upon one of the "finds" that are always so intriguing in uninhabited places. Under an aged *aromo*—even older than the trunk now standing, for the present tree grew as a sucker on a great dead stump—I stumbled over a long pile of stones that looked like a cairn heaped over a grave. Or it could have been a cache for treasure. Or could it have been only a bed or a bench? In any case, some person had piled up the stones—and he must have had some more than playful purpose, considering the work involved.

I had read somewhere—Darwin may have mentioned it—that on Santiago there were old stone benches built by the pirates. The Galápagos were a favourite hide-out of many well-known pirates in the seventeenth century—even Crusoe looked upon them once. I leaned toward the conclusion that this was one of those historical benches, though I liked the burial mound theory, too. It is a matter of history that an American naval lieutenant, named Cowan, was shot in a duel on Santiago in the year 1813 and was buried there.

I nosed among the stones, discovered and killed a few scorpions, and thought that I detected a smell of decay. Corpse under there? But no. The grave, if grave it was, could not be that new. Dead lizard or rat, perhaps—or just imagination. I moved away—I was beginning to get that queer feeling.

All along I had been kicking up pieces of red clay pottery. Presently I was walking in a little of it. I estimated the number of pieces, noted sizes and shapes. The shattered remains of at least fifty large jars were strewn over the flat.

Only someone who has been on a desert island alone can conceive how much a find like that, unimportant as it may have been, excited my imagination. Where had the jars come from? Who had broken them, and why? Could we use the pieces for anything?

Around four Ainslie returned to camp and reported that he had shovelled a half-ton of manure and old bones out of the spring bed and timed and measured the flow of water. The yield had been better than he had expected—nearly a quart an hour. He was encouraged about the water but still discouraged about the donkeys. They had not returned to the spring.

He went to the beach to bathe his sun-burned body and soak his legs in a tide pool. Then I gave him fresh bandages, omitting the cotton for it stuck to the sore spots and was very painful to remove. The burns had started to heal, but the salt-water treatment and the dressing would have to be repeated daily for at least a week.

D

That night two of the donkeys came down the canyon side with a clatter of hoofs and rolling stones. I nudged the sleeping Ainslie and said: "Burros!" He came to with difficulty, started to say a fighting word about donkeys who were always prowling around at night, and then, realising that luck had walked into our camp, he changed it to "Bless their brutish hearts!" He fumbled for a flashlight and a rope and burst into a stream of words and not a single word was a blessing. The old mare who was the leader of our donkey pack had knocked the cover off my bean kettle and had her muzzle deep in it. The younger donkey had torn open the camote sack and was crunching avidly.

"Let them finish the left-over beans—they are ruined, anyway," I said. "Then they will have memories to come home to."

"What left-over beans?"

When Ainslie went to the spring next morning, he carried his .22 slung over one shoulder and a heavy piece of roofing iron over the other. The donkeys walked ahead of him, unburdened. We had pack saddles for them and all the rest of the necessary trappings, but Ainslie said that while a donkey can easily carry two pieces of roofing, one on each side of the pack saddle, it is next to impossible to load him with a single piece. However, if Ainslie had been an Ecuadorian, one of the donkeys would have carried the roofing. The truth was that the *gringo* did not have the heart to work the little beasts yet—they were thin and tired and probably very thirsty.

He returned at noon, carrying a skinned and gutted goat, and said that the donkeys had drunk all the water in his catchment basin—about two bucketfuls. The third donkey had not been present.

During lunch I told him about the potsherds I had found on the flat—Pirate Flat we called it already.

"There are a lot more broken jars on the other side of the canyon too," he said. "Somebody really must have had a cracking good time breaking those pots."

Ainslie cut up the goat carcass in convenient cooking pieces and then went up on Pirate Flat. He stayed there so long that I wondered what he could be up to. Finally I went to see.

He was collecting the broken pieces and arranging them on a clean stretch of sandstone to form capital letters four feet high. His work, so far, consisted of the letters "O.K." complete with full stops.

"It can't be that you are just playing," I said after I had watched for a while.

"No, it can't be that," Ainslie answered and went on to build the letter B.

"What is that word going to be?" I asked. "And why is it going to be?"

"The word is going to be 'but'."

"You are spelling out a message to someone who might fly over the island, or you are hoping to contact heaven. Now which is it?"

"Well, I got to thinking that suppose the spring should

cease running and my proposed still did not work—then what? I remembered that the commanding officer at the air base told me to rig up some sort of signal, so that when he sent a plane over, the flyers could find out how we were doing. Now, if I can form the words 'O.K.—BUT VERY LITTLE WATER HERE NOW' and make them large enough to be read from a low-flying plane, the trick will be done. I'll also pile up enough wood to make a large fire, if that should prove desirable."

The next morning a cloud formed suddenly on Sugar Loaf and began spreading toward the beach. I covered the bedding and food sacks with sheets of roofing, and then it was raining —a cool, light shower. Water dripped from the grooves in the roofing—heavens, going to waste! And me with a washing in the clothes-bag. I put kettles, pans, cups, saucers—all the containers I had—under the drip, and watched anxiously, praying, actually praying, that the shower would last. It did last long enough to give me three gallons of rain water—not very clean, but, *gracios a Dios,* free of salt.

When Ainslie came home, I said: "They must have read your message Up There—or am I being irreverent as usual?"

"Oh, I don't know. They are not fools Up There. They can read. Why should a prayer spelled out with potsherds be more irreverent than one mumbled in a prophet's beard?"

VI. NO HOME LIKE OUR OWN

COMING upon us in our roofless camp in the gully, anyone with good sense would have asked immediately: "Why in the name of everything that is intelligent, didn't you bring a tent? You had learned previously at the dear school of experience what conditions you would face on Santiago. Or are there really people who never learn anything in any school whatever?"

We would have answered, smiling our superior smile: "We thought of bringing a tent, but thinking of it did not provide us with one." Then in our turn we would have asked: "Did you ever try shopping in Guayaquil?"

"But why not bring a tent from the States? There must have been mountains of army tents and other good camping equipment for sale in the United States, what with war surplus and all."

"Don't you know, my dear fellow, that passenger planes limit the weight of baggage to fifty pounds per person? We came from Vera Cruz to Quito by air, you know."

"Why didn't you come by ship? After all, anyone who comes on an expedition like this should think of all the possibilities and pick the best course for his purpose?"

"What year is this, brother?" we would have retorted. "We waited six months trying to get a reservation on a ship to Guayaquil. In that time, instead of working ourselves to the head of the list of those wanting reservations, we found ourselves farther from the top than we started. Diplomatic personnel, the agents said, and other people with special permits and priorities were always barging into the line ahead of us. It was either a trip by bus, train, and plane, or no trip at all for at least another year. And anyhow, what we did manage to bring suits our purposes better. As you so kindly pointed out, we have attended the dear school of experience. We were able to get corrugated iron roofing—at a price—in Guayaquil because the Guayaquileños must have that kind of roofing themselves for very much the same reasons as we. You can catch rain water from a 'tin roof' much better than from thatch or canvas—and consider how much longer it lasts."

But no one came to ask us questions or give us advice—though, heaven knows, we had had plenty of advice on everything at one time or another and profited by some of it. And we might have profited more had we taken more advice. On the other hand, we would not have came to Santiago at all, if we had listened to every bit of advice offered, in fact—we would not have come to the Galápagos. Good advice usually points in the direction of the well-travelled road, and that is not the direction adventure lies.

One drawback to the use of corrugated iron roofing as a rain shelter is that it must be supported by a frame. We had brought no lumber, though we had thought of that too—and not only thought, for Ainslie had made a down payment of two hundred *sucres* to a lumber dealer for the purchase of a thousand feet of frame and siding material and a dozen long poles of bamboo. At the last moment we had been told that the *Calderón* was to be so heavily loaded with lumber for some of the settlers on Santa Cruz and Isabela that she would have no room for ours. However, as it turned out, we did not really need lumber. Not having it meant more work for Ainslie—though, as he said, work was not a serious misfortune. To have no work would have been worse.

Before we arrived on Santiago we had planned to establish our living quarters somewhere near one of the springs—preferably the same pleasant spot we had occupied in 1937. But having discovered the jittery condition of the larger spring, we had concluded that the smaller one must be quite dry. Should we live at the Goya Rico spring then, with its five gallons a day, or on the beach? I went to the spring one morning to look that area over, and we decided against it, for the time, anyhow. The heavy brush which had once covered that region was dead now—even some of the trees had died and fallen—and I, for one, found the place depressing. Though it had one or two advantages—we could have a better garden up there than on the beach, the hot season would be less hot, and the view over the bay and Isabela was magnificent. At the beach, on the other hand, we would be more likely to contact visitors, if any came, and the ocean would afford recreation and entertainment. What little water there was could be carried down, for we had two donkeys, and perhaps three, for the little truant mare might decide to come home one day.

So, until circumstances forced us to move elsewhere or made other places more attractive, we elected to stay on the beach.

And the sandstone corral, a hundred yards up the canyon from the landing, was the natural house-site. The floor of the corral was already fairly level, the trees would give some much-needed shade, and the tufa wall, when repaired, would keep out animals, both wild and domestic. One unfavourable feature was apparent—when and if the heavy rains came, there would be a nasty wash down the canyon and right through our dooryard and perhaps even our house. But Ainslie, the engineer, thought he could take care of that by ditching and terracing. At the bottom of the canyon there was sufficient soil for a little garden—all we should need in the next few months and certainly all that our skimpy water resources allowed.

A week after our arrival, when his legs had healed sufficiently to make walking comfortable, Ainslie was back at his old trick of searching for *chala* poles and carrying them home on his shoulder. It took four days of searching and carrying to collect enough poles for a house frame fourteen by sixteen feet in area and eight feet high. Living *chala* poles, large enough to use for house-building, were rare on the flat now. Once the frame was up, it was a simple thing to put on the sheets of roofing—this was finished in less than an hour. During our first stay on Santiago we had roofed our *chala* pole *casucha* with bur-grass thatch, and that had been quite a different matter.

We unpacked our little white cots—English make, the Guayaquil dealer had assured us as we paid his inflated price—set them up under the new roof, made up the beds, arranged the mosquito nets, and for the first night in three weeks slept with a roof over our heads. That made us feel safe and settled. The next morning we awoke to Christmas. Santa Claus had completely forgotten us, but we deserved what we got. We had completely forgotten Santa Claus.

Or perhaps not so. The roof over our heads could have been a gift of the Magi, and there was something else too. In the night we were startled awake by a loud bang on the resounding iron roof and then a sound as if something with scratchy toes were walking on it. Followed a tattoo as on an iron drum head and a little later a long, raucous cry. Presently there was a windy "pop-pop-pop" as of beating wings.

I sat up with a half-conscious "Is it angel or devil?" But Ainslie was already on his feet and sending beams in all directions with the flashlight. On the corral floor the beam caught a gawky, dark-grey bird about twice the size of a crow, with a rather long neck and legs. Two long feathers hung down the back of his head—they might have been either white or yellow. The visitor was not startled by the beam of light, but strolled along leisurely looking about him as if he thought himself alone in the place.   He examined the ground and rocks beneath his feet, pecked at something a couple of times, seemed to catch and eat it.   Could he have been hunting geckos?   Of that I disapproved.   Finally he hopped up on the corral wall, paraded along it for a few minutes, and then made pop-pop-pop with his wings and landed on the roof again.

"Can this be good?" I asked Ainslie, who is daffy about birds, especially those he had never seen before.   "We want to catch water off the roof sometime, and I'm afraid our caller is not house-broken."

"But hold on a minute," counselled Ainslie softly, as he studied the bird in the beam of the flashlight.   "If I know anything about birds, this is a heron—the yellow-crowned night heron, I think.   And you know what the Chinese say."

"What of whatever the Chinese say?   All I know right now is that this *pajarote* makes a dreadful noise in the middle of a quiet night, and he probably intends to use our clean, new roof as a privy.   What say I take a stick to him?"

"No, not yet.   Not on his first visit, anyhow.   Evidently you don't know your Chinese proverbs."

"Out with your proverb then, or it's out with the bird."

"A heron on the roof is an omen of good fortune."

Good fortune, was it?   And on Christmas Eve, too.   I looked on the nonchalant bird with greater interest.   "Okay," I told him, "bring your good fortune then, for we can use it, but, mind you, bring nothing else—or else!"

The bird gave one of his raucous cries, pop-pop-popped with his wings, and was off toward the beach, from where he had heard another similar cry pitched in a somewhat higher key. He returned the next night and on many other nights, especially when there was a moon.   We could not resent his visits too much—after all, we had some respect for the wisdom of the Chinese and also some respect for the bird's individual rights. Evidently we had built our house in his canyon.

We spent the Fiesta del Nacimiento making improvements on the house.   Having those possible rains in mind, Ainslie raised the level of the floor a foot above the canyon bottom with earth and a layer of flat sandstone blocks.   I finished the floor with six Indian reed mats, and Ainslie lined the edges, where the walls should have been, with rows of packing-boxes.   These boxes were filled with cans of flour and beans and other things, and arranged along the "wall" this way, they were easy to get into. We nailed reed mats on the southern and eastern exposures for wind and sun protection, and stacked three empty packing-boxes between the heads of the beds to make a table and shelves. I had bought coarse-woven, red-striped ticking in Guayaquil for bedspreads, pillows, and shelf-curtains, and when I dressed the *casucha* with these, the result was all that a reasonable desert islander could have asked. I do not mean to imply that we were entirely reasonable. For one thing, we wished for a screen-walled house. Oh, yes, we had thought of screen, too, and had actually bought some good copper screen, but there was not enough of it to make four walls without the help of siding to fill in. "And why not more screen?" you ask. "Shortages," is our answer—"both of money and screen." It was scarce and appallingly expensive in Guayaquil.

While Ainslie had been building the house, I had filled the gaps in my working time by pulling up and stacking the dead brush and weeds inside the corral and in the part of the canyon that was now our front yard. Within a week I had seven great heaps of brush ready to burn. This work was not unpleasant, for I like to see results, and results are always easy to see after a good cleaning job. But my skin suffered, as did Ainslie's on his *chala* and water-carrying expeditions. We were already sun-burned and even tanned from our stay in Guayaquil and the sea voyage on the shadeless deck of the *Calderón*, but the sun-burn we got on our rock-ribbed *playa* was like nothing we had pre-viously experienced—except, of course, the deep burns on Ainslie's legs. Though we wore long sleeves, long trousers, and wide-brimmed monte-cristi hats of the type Ecuadorian work-men wear in the hot season of the coastal regions, we felt seared and toasted after each hour away from the shade. And even good sun-glasses that had cost us six dollars a pair in Oakland seemed to give inadequate protection to the eyes. It was not really hot yet, for the south-east trades were still blowing in December, and they are always fresh in the Galapagos region, but the canyon walls cut off some of the breeze and also absorbed and reflected the sun's rays. The brilliance of the light was what worked the damage.

"Get used to it," we urged each other. "We did it before." The advice was good, but our hides toughened at their own slow pace, and no amount of willing seemed to hurry the process.

The very worst spot for me was beside the cooking fire at

noon. Ainslie had built the provisional fireplace against the western slope of the gully and the blinding sun beat against the dry sandstone all morning. By noon heat radiated from the slope as from an old-style base-burner stove. With the radiation from both the fire and the canyon side to the front and the heat and light of the sun on the back, daytime cooking there was all but intolerable.

So I spoke for a better-situated fireplace as the next, very next, "must do" task.

At the front entrance of the corral stood a couple of *muyuyus*, partially covered with leaves. Near-by was an *aromo* which also cast a thin but acceptable shade. Under the *muyuyus* and next to the spot where Ainslie planned to construct a neat gateway and make a few stone steps, for the corral floor was higher than the canyon bottom to the front, Ainslie began building a really professional fireplace. He even consulted a book of designs which included a few outdoor fireplaces and barbecue pits. He had bought the book in San Francisco with just such a use for it in mind.

Ainslie piled up the sandstone blocks to form a flat-topped fireplace about three feet wide and six feet long, and incorporated it into the corral wall so that it seemed part of it. Luckily Nature had put this sedimentary rock down in cracked layers, of an even thickness—not more than four inches, which made it easy to pry up with a pick and trim with a hatchet. Ainslie was so careful a stonemason that he used a level in fitting the blocks in place. He left a firebox two feet square and a foot deep—which, when I put it to use, turned out to be too large, and we had to fill it partially with more blocks. Over the firebox he laid an iron grill, made to order for him by a Guayaquil blacksmith. He also left a foot-deep kindling niche near the bottom. For the top layer of stones, which would serve me as a cooking table, Ainslie carried in several perfectly flat pieces some three square feet in area. These he found a quarter of a mile from camp, and when I suggested that he let one of the burros carry them, he said that the sandstone was so friable and those perfect pieces so precious that he could not trust them to the donkeys.

The fireplace and the "gate-posts" and steps next it having been completed, the rest of the stone wall could wait for later repairs and completion. Ainslie worked on it just enough to discourage our lady-of-leisure donkeys from entering the corral at night or in our absence, and blocked up the back entrance with poles and brush. The front gate could be closed by rolling one of the empty oil drums against it. In our first efforts to make the place donkey-proof we were more hopeful than realistic, for the first time we left it unoccupied for half an hour, the donkeys came in by jumping the wall and ate ten of our twenty pounds of crackers. These *galletas* were in a covered tin, and there was a pile of blankets on the cover, but our donkeys were Ecuadorian educated and knew how to nose out and dig up food. They were not starving either, for we gave them corn every day and they were already fatter and sleeker than they had been when we bought them.

Between the house and the fireplace we now had a perfect *patio*. Three *aromos* shaded it, and Ainslie filled in and levelled the floor. To one side he lined up four of our empty oil drums —the tops had been cut off and they had been painted green with two white stripes, just as Ainslie had ordered in Guayaquil. Into these fifty-five gallon drums we put all the provisions that had come in sacks—sugar, rice, corn, potatoes, onions, garlic, and some of the beans. The rest of the beans, as well as the peas, lentils, raw peanuts, and a quintal of flour had been packed and transported in five-gallon gasoline tins with removable covers— these covers too had been made to order by a Guayaquil tin-smith. The Ecuadorians are good at this sort of work. On opening the corn sacks we found that all four quintals were shrivelled, mouldy, and infested with weevils. We should have insisted on having the sacks opened before we bought them— any Guayaquileño would have taken this precaution as a matter of course. However, not much was lost—the corn would do for the animals and it had been relatively cheap. I was afraid—in fact, I knew—that the weevils would spread into the rice, but I put on my optimistic blinkers, for the task of sunning four hundred pounds of corn at that busy time was appalling. Naturally, I saved myself no work. I sunned four hundred pounds of rice a few weeks later.

Ainslie covered the drums with one heavy, flat piece of galvanised iron some seven by three feet in size. This made an excellent table to hold the water buckets or whatever else we cared to place on it. Neither rain nor rats could enter the food drums now, though ants could get into the sugar. Fortunately few ants were around and they seemed timid and harmless.

Next to the drums, under a small *aromo*, Ainslie built a sort of stone altar and on this he placed three packing-boxes to form a dish cupboard. All except one of our boxes were gasoline boxes, made to hold two five-gallon rectangular tins. This size was convenient to handle and use for whatever purpose we found for them—also they had been convenient to buy in Guayaquil. In front of the cupboard I tacked a curtain of the same red-striped material I had used for the bedspreads.

We had one large packing-box, about four feet by two, and Ainslie made a dining-table of the bottom half by nailing four *chala* legs on it. The remaining portion of the box made two benches. These we set up under our best *aromo* tree, and the *patio* was ready to receive company.

The work of building living quarters did not end with the completion of the house and the al fresco kitchen. There were still many days of levelling the ground all around the house, digging drainage ditches—of all things, in this parched place— along the sides of the levelled area, and pruning the graceless or dead limbs of the *aromos* and *muyuyus*. Behind the house was a tangled, matted, rat-harbouring thicket of vines and thorn-bushes—strange that in this desert of tufa so many things should grow after all, and grow so tough and strong. Ainslie worked two afternoons cleaning this out. And weeks of work on the corral wall still remained, though Ainslie did not realise when he started this task that he would develop a compulsion to tear all the original construction apart and rebuild the wall about as carefully as he had built the fireplace. And he had to make it three feet high to keep the donkeys from jumping over it. When completed, from the direction of the beach the place looked like a fortress.

We felt that we ought to have a good name for our beach house, something snappy like Dorothy Parker's "Rising Gorge." But that was such a high level to aim at that we could not do it. "Heron's Rest," "World's End," and "Conway Castle," did not seem quite witty enough. After discussing the business for a couple of hours one evening, we gave up, and found ourselves calling the place "El Corral" the next day. El Corral it remained.

All this construction work took longer than my brief tale of it would indicate, for Ainslie spent each morning at the spring, where he was still cleaning out deposits of dung and sediment and piling up and burning dead brush. And every time there was a light rain—which happened on the average once a week at this season—dirty surface water washed into the catchment basin and it had to be emptied and all the water given to the donkeys or used for washing clothes—if it was clean enough for washing. Then the hole had to be wiped clean. Ainslie was

extra finicky about his water source—he did not want me even
to see it until he had worked for a week on the place.

So much earth and animal droppings had to be moved from
the immediate vicinity of the water-hole that Ainslie thought
up a good use for them. He began to build a completely hand-
made garden plot below the spring—a small garden only thirty
feet square, but fully three feet deep with the finest soil in the
world. This involved some stone work too, for he had to build

a retaining wall on two sides to keep the rains from washing the
soil down the gully. Then, to allow the sun to reach the projected garden, Ainslie cleared out some of the still living brush
and a couple of old *muyuyus,* and pruned the other trees which
grew comparatively large in this spot where water was evidently
available below the surface of the ground. We had enough barb-
wire to fence this small garden well, though posts would be
another backache.

In the course of his digging, Ainslie found two other catchment basins a couple of yards below the first one. These basins
were apparently very old and yielded no water, and we could
not guess who had dug them—perhaps some of our pirates.
Farther down the gully from these basins were the remains of

a dam made of tree trunks and stones. It was just this dam, very likely, that had caused the sand and earth to pile up in the gully above it. Ainslie removed the dam—it was better to let the overflow—if there should ever be an overflow again—run down the gully and so keep the spring bed clean.

The trail to the spring was easily passable and not difficult for a moderately observant person to follow—wild donkeys and goats had seen to that. But it was not good enough for Ainslie. He figured that he would eventually save time and steps if he surveyed a straight road, cleared it of what brush the dry years had left, and built up with slag, lava and tufa, the old dilapidated fill made years ago by salt miners to facilitate the crossing of a wide gully. This work was not at all necessary to us from the point of view of mere existence, and it was not the sort of sport most people care to undertake for pastime or pleasure. They would rather go hunting for animals they don't need for food or can't eat, anyway, or angle for fish just because they hope to land a swordfish or wahoo bigger than anybody else has ever landed. To them Ainslie's road building would have seemed quite senseless. And I confess that it sometimes seemed senseless to me too, though I could not get Anislie to look at it from my side.

Ainslie loves to "make improvements"—a strange passion in a man who also loves to live in "unimproved" places where Nature has had her way undisturbed for ages, and a haphazard and slovenly way it can seem to a man who has a precise, constructive streak in him. I imagine that every time Ainslie comes upon a really cluttered-up and wild place he immediately begins planning roads, terraces, clearing and pruning jobs, and says to himself: "Just think what I could do to this mess!" He never considers the cost in labour or headaches any more than the lion hunter considers it. In fact, to him as to the others, the more difficulty there is, the more sport. Though I doubt that Ainslie ever thinks of himself as a sportsman.

And Ainslie always thinks of the other fellow—that is, the other fellow's comfort and convenience and also his approval. "Look upon my works," he says inwardly and perhaps unconsciously, "and be impressed and astounded!" How like a man —or a woman or a child! Show me a person who does not like approving "ohs" and "ahs" from his fellow creatures and I think you will show me a dead man. So it is not the man in general that is different in Ainslie's case—it is the particular kind of activity that pleases him and with which he likes to please and astonish other people. Very few men find those satisfactions in building a road "from nowhere to nowhere in no-man's-land for no reason."

The words were mine. Ainslie answered them by planning still more improvements on the road. He aimed to make it absolutely foolproof. No one must possibly get lost in the spring trail—not even I. I am a poor follower of trails and directions, not because I am entirely unobservant but because I have the habit of observing irrelevant things. On a strange trail I pass up the signs—there are always signs that a good woodsman can read no matter how signless the terrain may seem to the novice—for I get interested in birds, plants, rocks, and oddities, or get lost in my own reveries. Ainslie also had in mind other persons who might, by aim, chance, or accident, find themselves on the island and in need of water. He could not forget how well covered up the water source had been when we landed on Santiago this second time.

When I made my first trip to the spring alone with my washing in a bag over my shoulder, I missed the trail, though I found it again soon enough by the smoke of a fire Ainslie happened to have made that day to burn brush. On the way back I made little road marks along the ambiguous places— ambiguous to me, that is—by piling three or four stones on top of each other at regular intervals.

A week later, when there was washing water in the hole again, I found Ainslie at work on the trail. He was building a little tower about four feet high of tufa blocks. Ahead I could see two similar towers, a few rods apart, lined up on the side of the trail.

"Mysterious are thy designs," I greeted him, "and thy ways past finding out."

"If trail signs were not so mysterious to you, and roadways past finding out, I would not be doing this," he smart-alecked back.

"But I made myself some road signs and I am following them now."

"And as soon as the rains come and the brush and grass grow up, where will your little signs be?"

"I can find the way all right by directing my march toward that black cone of volcanic sand on the side of Sugar Loaf. The spring is in the clump of trees near it. Or don't you know?"

'I guess you could find it now that you know exactly where to look. But suppose you were a stranger here and thirsty?"

"But how is a stranger to know that these towers have any-thing to do with water?"

"He won't. But he will be curious. I'll build these towers, as you call them, all along the trail close enough together so that you can see at least one other tower in either direction from each of them. If a thirsty person should find himself on the island he would follow the towers out of curiosity, if for no other reason, and come to the water-hole. Are my designs so mysterious now?"

"And you could carve the word WATER on the side of the spring canyon with an arrow pointing toward the water-hole. That would be helpful if the hole should get filled up again."

"If I get around to it, I'll do that too. And you are not the first to think of it, so don't go getting big ideas."

"And you could take some of those potsherds or tufa slabs and build the word WATER near the beach, with an arrow pointing up the trail. That would really cinch it."

Ainslie thought a while. Evidently that idea had not occurred to him. Then he said: "It would cinch out all the romance and adventure, too. I think I am against that pro-position."

Months later the towers were all up. They were constructed of wide, flat slabs at the bottom and smaller ones at the top, and from a distance they looked like a procession of brown, wide-skirted Andean women on their way to market. We called them our "Quechua Ladies." At twilight the illusion was almost convincing even to us. We could imagine how easily they could mystify a stranger.

I had a piece of work at home which matched, after a fashion, Ainslie's work project at the spring. I was making little garden spots—dots I called them. On the canyon bottom to the front of El Corral, from which I had cleaned out and burned the brush, I made pumpkin, melon, and cucumber hills. These hills had to be built several yards apart to prevent my hoped-for fruits from coming out "bastards"—that is the correct scientific word—and near the sides of the canyon where the bottom was a little higher, to keep the hills from being washed out to sea in a heavy rain. I dug up eight dots, each about three feet in diameter, probing the earth to a depth of at least a foot to locate rocks and pry them out. Then to each hill I carried about four gallons of old donkey manure from deposits I found on the flat. My carrying vessel was a large, shallow basin with handles, which the Ecuadorians call a *baila*. It was hand-hammered and shaped

YOUNG GALÁPAGOS HAWKS ON NEST

BOOBY ON NEST

from a piece cut out of an oil drum.   These utensils, handwork
and all, are very common and cheap in Ecuador.   I mixed the
manure with the earth, heaped each bed higher than the canyon
bottom, and made a tufa wall about a foot high around it to
hold the earth in.   In a dry place it is better to make vegetable
"hills" lower than the surrounding earth, to hold water; but,
paradoxically, I had both drought and flood to consider.   I made
few hills because we had only a little waste water to spare for
them, and I made them high to keep the rainy-season gully wash
from flooding them.

Before I sowed any seeds in the dots I kept giving them a
little water each day, one at a time—sometimes this water was
too soapy to be good for even pumpkins—until the soil was
moist for a few inches down.   Then I put in the seeds, planting
first one hill of cucumbers and then a hill of pie pumpkins.   We
had chosen these vegetables because they are sun-loving—though
they love water too—and because they had been very productive
when we raised them on Floreana previously.   However, I
planned to have only two pumpkin hills and two cucumber hills,
and save the other four for water-melons, which would be sown
last.   The little stone wall served for picturesqueness and to discourage the chickens, and I intended to pile some dry brush
over the hills after the seeds had sprouted, to hide the young
plants from finches as well as chickens.   Donkeys would be
another menace to the growing vines, and I could see myself
doing a lot of watching and chasing.   I estimated that we would
have enough water to keep the tiny plants alive until the rains
came—in February, we hoped.

Inside the corral, behind the house, I made a vegetable bed
about ten feet square, spading it up, digging out the stones, and
adding manure, as I had done for the dots.   I built this bed
up a little too, and gave it a low wall of stones, which Ainslie
improved when he found the time.   In this bed I planted
roquette, leaving room for ten tomato plants which I meant to
set out later.

I have never seen roquette growing in the United States,
never found it for sale in any market, never eaten it except when
I picked it out of my own Galápagos garden.   Yet the seeds I
planted came from the United States, so it must be grown there
somewhere.   Roquette is a plant that resembles mustard, though
the leaves are smoother in texture.   The leaves have a pleasant,
piquant flavour when eaten tender and uncooked, and taste very
much like mustard or turnip greens when cooked.

E

Incidentally, we could not have chosen a more satisfactory vegetable for our tiny garden in El Corral. We cannot say that it saved our lives, for our lives were not in danger—or not in any more danger than life always is, for only the dead are absolutely safe. But it helped to make life livable, and that is high praise. I seeded the roquette directly into the soil where it was to grow, for I was afraid transplanting would retard it, and gave it a panful of water in which I had previously washed my feet. It happened to rain a little the following night, and in a week I had three dozen plantlets—tiny and tender they were, but how they could take it! On some sunny afternoons they looked quite dead, but they revived again in the night. "Whenever I plant a garden, from now on," I promised them, "I'll always sow roquette out of pure gratitude."

Here and there in the canyon bottom I buried papaya, royal palm, and poinciana seeds just to see what would happen to them. I sowed more papaya seeds in an old washpan I had picked up on the Goya Rico beach and tomato seeds in a cup. We had plenty of other seeds—flower and vegetable seeds from the States and tree and shrub seeds from Guayaquil—but we saved these for later planting. Some of the tree seeds we planned to sow in the mountains when we made a trip up there, not with any idea of caring for the seedlings but just to give them that one chance in ten thousand they might have of growing up as wild trees.

Ainslie said that the only man-planted trees he knew of in the mountains were two immense avocado trees, sown there many years ago by some unknown benefactor. He also told me of a marine lieutenant who had been stationed at Baltra in the early days of the war and who had developed a passion for the Galápagos and dreamed of living on them some day. The starry-eyed youngster had gone about with seeds in his pockets, and whenever he was on land that looked in the least promising he has scattered lemon, orange, avocado, and other fruit tree seeds. This was an excellent practice in the Galápagos, where many fruit trees have grown up wild from just such planting but the lieutenant's timing was not so good. He should have sown his seeds about a hundred years ago when the islands were not yet stocked with hogs. There were perhaps thousands of hogs—originally of the domestic breeds but now wild for generations—in the Santiago mountains too. If they had not been there to eat up all the avocado seeds produced by the two big trees, our mountains might now be carrying a forest of avocado trees and perhaps oranges and lemons, for it was likely that those seeds too had been dropped there at some time by galápago hunters or chance adventurers.

So our hope of getting any trees eventually from our scattered seeds was exceedingly optimistic, though we were supported by the thought that hogs don't eat all kinds of seeds and seedlings. Guavas would have managed a foothold there, hogs or no hogs, but we had been very careful not to bring guava seeds to Santiago. In the Galápagos guavas have a tendency to take over the place, and they are almost hopelessly difficult to eradicate once they are established. Even so, I wished I had brought some guava seeds, without Ainslie's knowledge, for I like guavas, and to me, any fruit trees, no matter how vital and avid for *lebensraum*, are better than no fruit trees at all.

In the meantime life went on for us with its usual round from breakfast to dinner. (Even the unusual had happened—we had had visitors, but that is another story.) There was cooking, cleaning, washing, burro and chicken tending, fishing, hunting —about two-thirds of my time and a third of Ainslie's went into these. Ainslie's fundamental chores were bringing home two buckets of water each day when the water-hole was clean, fishing about once a week, and killing a goat twice a week. I say "killing" instead of "hunting," for killing was all his hunting amounted to as a general thing. The dog had soon learned to do the finding and catching.

Though hunting was so simple, now and then Ainslie and the dog did not find the right kind of animal, for they were choosy, but always they found something, either living or lifeless. One day, about two months after the house was completed, they came home without game, but Ainslie was carrying a weathered piece of lumber, sixteen feet long, on his shoulder. At one end of the two-by-four was a four-foot crosspiece and some faded rags hung from it.

"Now what?" I asked with my usual curiosity.

"I found a cross," answered Ainslie.

"You mean someone had been crucified?"

"Well, not exactly. Though I am reminded of the time my little friend Doyle carried the cross."

I said no more. I knew the story would come out sooner if I pretended no further interest.

"When they were surveying these islands while the base was being built, Doyle was with a party of engineers on Hood Island. Some three miles from the beach which was the base of operations rose a low, bristling crater, and the boss engineers decided to put a datum point on it. Now a datum point might be a little pyramidal 'tower', built of several long two-by-fours, or one upright two-by-four with a crosspiece, like this one that I found near Goya Rico Beach. Little Doyle, as the lowest ranking of the party, was elected to carry the 'cross' to the top of the crater.

"As the party clambered along that *playa* of lava boulders and cursed their way through the typical Hood Island thorny entanglements, which are no easier to pass through than barb-wire barriers, the big shots went ahead at their own unburdened pace, while Doyle struggled in the rear with the sixteen-foot cross on his shoulder. The three-mile stretch took two hours, and Doyle reached the top with his tongue hanging out and more than crowned with thorns—he was scratched and literally stuck-over with thorns from head to foot like a pin-cushion. From then on he referred to the crater as 'Golgotha' and to his expedition as 'Carrying the Cross'."

"And now that you have taken to carrying the cross, what are you going to do with it?"

"Well, there must be more of these crosses and perhaps a couple of 'towers' along the beach here or on top of some of the craters. Santiago was surveyed too. If I find the others, and I think I know where to look, I will have enough two-by-fours to make a new frame for the house. I don't like those *chala* poles—they look too crooked and flimsy."

"More work for you, and how!"

"Yes, but the improvement in the house will be worth it."

"Once you locate the crosses, you can saddle up the burros and make them carry the lumber, *verdad*?"

"No, the pieces are too long." As usual, there was an excuse for the donkeys.

Ainslie found another cross that afternoon on Pirate Point it had fallen down, or we would have found it sooner.

The following Sunday we walked to Ainslie's favourite fishing spot less than a mile to the west of our canyon, and not getting any fish in the first twenty minutes nor caring to wait for them any longer, we took off to explore an old crater near-by, which we called Red Mountain, because it was made of red slag. Skirting the *palo santo* covered flat at its base and looking for a good place to climb up to the rim, I saw something that at first seemed to be a dead tree, broken and fallen over half-way up the trunk. When I pointed it out to Ainslie and he had given it a good scrutiny, he concluded that it was a surveyor's "tower." We climbed up to see—the crater side was only about a hundred feet high and not very steep at that point—and sure enough, there was a tower.

"How do you expect to get this down?" I asked.

"Easy. I'll bring a hammer tomorrow, pull out the nails, and drop the pieces down the mountain-side. That may damage them a little but not too much if I choose a good place."

When those pieces of lumber had come home on Ainslie's shoulder within the following week, we did not yet have enough lumber for the new house frame.

"I have a hunch about where there is another tower," Ainslie said. "You know that old red crag at the lower end of the lava flow? If I know anything about surveying, the top of that crag is a good place for a datum point. I'll go see to-morrow."

"But won't you have a heck of a time carrying it—and you will need to make at least two trips if you find a tower. Carrying a cross over that stormy sea of lava, for half a mile at least, is something I wouldn't wish on the devil."

"I'd rather carry it across this lava flow where there are no thorny bushes than do it Doyle's way, and he was only half my size."

From the top of the flat I could see Ainslie as he took off over the lava from the nearer edge beside Goya Rico Beach. All I could see was a white speck, which was his wide monte-cristi hat, moving across the black horror. I lost sight of him behind a high black "wave" before he reached the crag. A couple of hours later I went up to look again, hoping to see him returning across the lava—the sun was blinding and there was a stiffish breeze, which I thought would hamper him. But when I caught sight of Ainslie he was already on the flat to my side of the Goya Rico Beach, and he had a load of lumber on his shoulder.

"Well, I found a tower, as I had expected, and I also found something else," he said when he had laid two sixteen-foot two-by-fours on the ground beside the gate.

I had visions of graves and treasure and human skeletons at the mention of "Something else," but I asked no questions this time. As you may have noticed, Ainslie makes indirect answers to direct questions.

"That crag is really two crags, though it looks like one from here. The lava flowed through between them. And on one of the crags—it seems to be a small crater—is a salt-water pool. I tasted the water to make sure."

"Another salt pool? Is that all? Now there are four we know of in this region. Why don't you find a fresh-water pool sometime?"

"Yes, why don't I? Though a fresh-water pool on top of that crag would do us little good."

When Ainslie had made one more trip to the red crag and

I had jittered at home expecting him to drag back with a broken leg or never drag back at all, he had collected all the datum points in our vicinity—and they yielded just enough lumber to make the house-frame, the skeleton of a screen-covered box for keeping meat, and a few scraps of kindling wood. He designed, measured, and sawed the pieces for the frame before he put any of them up. Then, one day when all the parts were ready and no rain clouds were in sight, he took the sheets of roofing off the *chala* frame, tore it apart, set the old poles carefully aside for later use, nailed up the new frame, and arranged the roofing in place. Everything had been completed by evening.

Though the new house was no larger than the old one, it looked more spacious, and the lines were straight. In one way,

I liked the "improvement" less than the original—the colour of the *chala* poles had harmonised beautifully with the trunks of the *aromos* near-by, and the weathered grey of the imported fir, though not at all ugly, was nevertheless not quite so artistic. It lacked the flecks of lichen that gave a faultless finish to the *chala* bark—and, on second thought, were those machine-sawed angles better than haphazard curves? Ainslie said they were.

VII. HAPPY HUNTING GROUNDS

THERE may have been neurotics among the cave-men—in fact, I am of the opinion that there were—though it is generally believed that neuroses are modern developments brought on by maladjustments of the individual to situations that change too rapidly, do not change rapidly enough, change in the wrong direction, or do not change at all. Anyway, the neurotic is not getting what he craves, or he is getting too much of it, or he does not know what he craves, or he thinks he knows and happens to be wrong. His situation is so unsettled and its elements jump about so fast in all directions that he himself does not know in what direction to jump, or, if he knows, he cannot jump fast enough.

The savage is supposed to be so much at home in his perfectly balanced element that he is never at a loss. He always knows which way to jump. And he is supposed to know just what he wants, and he is supposed to get it, just fast enough and in the right quantities. His wants are simple and his methods of satisfying them direct and certain. Something of this savage directness and simplicity is believed to lurk in the dark depths of the minds of all of us—especially the males—no matter how many generations we have lived with subways, water closets, and such "breakfast foods" as "Pep," "Kicks," and "Cheerios." And a return to this basic "natural" state is supposed to produce a condition of perfect serenity and bliss in the human individual.

According to reports I have heard, the hunter of the mammoth or the sabre-tooth desired few things—drink, meat, sport, sufficient warmth to keep him from losing his toes, safe sleeping, and sex. All these he must have got, of course, or he would not have lived long enough to beget generations of deer-and-wild-boar-hunters, who in their turn begat our nearer, work-and-money-hunting ancestors.

I admit that the cave-dweller had an easier time deciding what he wanted than we moderns—all he had to do was follow his senses and "instincts." His belly told him when he needed to eat, his skin spoke when he needed to seek warmth. He did not have to stay awake nights trying to decide whether to buy a

Ford or a Cadillac, or whether to buy neither and pay off the mortgage on the house instead. His nights were troubled only by the hungry screams of sabre-tooths and his cave-baby yelling for a dry bearskin. But these were not new and constantly changing worries—to him sabre-tooths and bawling babies were of the things that ever had been and ever would be, world without end.

While the Conways did not live in a cave, though they would have welcomed one, and had been subjected to the hazards and vicissitudes of civilisation for many years, they found themselves pretty much in the same situation as the cave-man. We could get all the good things that the cave-man craved, and many of them we got in much the same way. Some things our island provided automatically. The climate, while it sometimes made us shiver a little or burn a little, gave us a very liveable environment, and we had no worries about safe sleeping, for there were no man-eating night prowlers on Santiago. The sex problem too was automatically solved; we had had the foresight to be born of opposite sexes. The matter of drink, also, was not too painful a question; nature gave us water, though we had to scratch some to find it and keep it running. And having brought with us many of the things desired by civilised man, meat and sport were the only things left for the fundamental man in us to worry about. If the civilised man in us craved more than we had provided for him—and he did—that is a subject for another day. Right now we are primitive men, hunting meat.

Meat hunting and sport are a married pair and I do not intend to divorce them. To the primitive man, whether a cave-dweller or a Rotarian in the deer season, hunting is sport as well as meat getting. Even the sport of war, which savages of any era seem to love, may have begun as food hunting—perhaps all savages were once cannibals, and they started hunting men in order to eat them. War, without the subsequent feast on the victims, is perhaps one of the first indications of approaching civilisation.

With us, meat and sport were also joined—and I include fish with meat for the sake of logic and brevity. If we got less kick out of our hunting than the savage presumably did, we could blame that shortcoming on the years we had spent in cities and other unnatural places and on the innocence and defencelessness of our game.

I count myself in on Ainslie's hunting and fishing activities though I hardly ever went with Ainslie when he took off across the flat with gun and dog or with rod and hook. That is, I did not walk with him, step for step, or shoot or capture the quarry. But I always went along mentally, carrying my worries with me, and each time Ainslie returned, he gave me a detailed description of the chase. He seemed to like telling me and I liked to hear. There was so little else to tell or hear in our household. Sometimes I was able to observe part of the operations—hear the shot, if shot there was, hear the dog barking, see the catch being carried home, skinned, gutted, and carved. My rôle in respect to hunting was that of the typical cave-woman, I suppose, as Ainslie's was that of the cave-man and the dog's was that of the cave-dog.

When Ainslie started out with the hope or intention of finding a goat—or whenever he started out with any intention at all—he was dressed in his customary Santiago costume, boxer-style underdrawers or khaki pants cut down to a few inches above the knee, sneakers, a *jipijapi* hat (just another name for the monte-cristi or misnamed panama), sun-glasses, and nothing more. He carried a coil of rope over his bare, mahogany-coloured shoulder, or a gun, or both. At his belt he had a hunting knife. Tucked in his belt he also carried sometimes a little muslin sack I had designed purposely as a "*manteca* sack." This was to receive, and keep clean, any fat the hoped-for catch might have.

In hunting goats Ainslie generally followed one of two procedures—either he hunted with the rope and the dog on his morning excursions to the spring or his work on the road, or he went out an hour before sunset with the gun and without the dog—the dog had to be tied up, or she would have gone whether she was invited or not. This evening hunting was usually inspired by one of two things—he had not been successful in the morning, or he happened to see some very tempting goats very close to El Corral.

He did not take the gun in the morning, as a rule, because he did not kill his goats so early in the day—he merely caught them with the aid of the dog, tied them to a tree with the rope he carried, and returned late in the afternoon to do the butchering. This was not so unkind to the tethered goats as it might seem —usually the prisoner's buddies came to stand or take a siesta under the tree with him. Sometimes Ainslie killed the goat on the spot where he had been tied, left the hide, guts, and head there for the hawks and rats, and carried the clean carcass home on his shoulder. Oftener, however, he persuaded his catch to travel home on his own four nimble legs and butchered him not too far from camp. Ainslie saved his back this way, though his legs and arms got some rough exercise if the goat happened to be especially wild or stubborn.

This sounds very simple, and generally it was very simple to catch our kind of game—the beasts were numerous and not really wild. And we had an excellent dog. She was not yet quite full-grown, but in spite of her puppy ways, she was intelligent and tractable. As soon as she learned to understand Ainslie's commands—which he was considerate enough to speak in Spanish—she cheerfully risked her life to obey them. Ainslie taught her to follow at his heels—though she could not resist dashing off to chase lizards every two minutes and had to be called back—and not run after goats until he had given her the word. Left to her own discretion, she would have picked the biggest, smelliest bucks she could find—or failing to find them—some poor, hard-working doe with two kids.

Ainslie wanted fat, kidless does or young goats of either sex. The first preference went to the fat barren doe because she had plenty of fine-flavoured meat and six or seven pounds of good cooking fat. We could have got more meat from a full-grown buck, but practically no fat, and all too much aroma and flavour. And Ainslie did not care for the fighting qualities of bucks, though they would have added zest to the sport—had he hunted only twice a year instead of twice a week, he might have changed his taste. A buck is not so willing to be caught by the horns as a doe or kid, nor is he as willing to run to the butchering spot at the end of a rope. The little added zest, Ainslie figured, was not worth the added charley-horses in his muscles or the bruises on his skin. Had there been a shortage of game it would have been wiser practice to spare the does and eat only bucks, but there was no shortage—an overabundance rather.

Though three old, long-whiskered bucks clearly asked for it. Their favourite pasture ground was in the neighbourhood of El Corral, and we saw them every day, either grazing on the spare grass of Pirate Point where they often skirted so close to the edge of the cliff that I worried—quite needlessly, of course—about their safety, or standing on their hind legs against a *monte salado* or *aromo* tree, reaching for leaves or tender shoots. They became so familiar that we had to name them; Los Hermanos Negros, they were called, or The Black Brothers. As time went on, the Hermanos and the dog developed a feud, and often black dog and black goats mixed in such noisy frays that they seemed like black demons celebrating some infernal holiday. So Los Hermanos Negros ended as strips of jerky—not all at once, but each in turn. The dog ate most of the meat, as perhaps she deserved.

The dog and Ainslie were pretty sure of getting whichever animal they went after, though not always. One morning on the way to the spring they startled a bunch of does and kids who seemed to have a pre-arranged place of refuge in mind. These candidates for survival, instead of taking off hysterically in any old direction, headed straight for the ocean. Followed by the dog, they scrambled out on a point of tide-washed rocks and stood there with their rumps toward the sea. The dog harried them but could not get a throat-hold—the waves kept washing her off her feet. Ainslie called the dog off, and left the goats on their rock. Late in the afternoon Ainslie and I went out to see if the high tide had drowned the refugees or if they had gone away. They were still there, firm on their rock, though the incoming breakers sometimes submerged them and the foaming sea rioted between them and the land. They seemed to know that the water would not rise quite high enough to drown them. How they kept their foothold only a goat knows.

Ainslie had a few goat-catching expeditions that gave him all the sport even an avid sportsman could have wanted. One day he and the dog were trying to round up a young doe on Pirate Flat, not far from the cliff overlooking the ocean. As the hunters approached, the doe suddenly disappeared. The dog sniffed about a few minites, puzzled, and then she too disappeared. There was some shrubbery in the way and Ainslie could not see what had happened to either of the animals.

Then he heard the dog barking—somewhere out at sea, it seemed. Ainslie walked to the edge of the cliff, scanned the ocean, but saw nothing except sea birds and water. The dog now seemed to be barking somewhere beneath his feet. He knelt on the edge of the barranca and peered down. The dog was on a tiny bar of sand beneath the cliff, looking up and barking. Evidently she had dashed along the edge of the cliff and down a slope leading to the ocean. But where was the goat?

Ainslie leaned over the cliff a little farther—it still gives me the willies to think of it—and there, on a tiny ledge of sandstone, some three by six feet in area, were four goats—the doe he had been hunting, another doe, and two kids. The ledge was perhaps six feet below Ainslie and thirty feet above the water, and the cliff was perpendicular and sheer. The goats seemed quite at peace on their narrow shelf—and why not? The dog could not reach them there.

Ainslie must have been in one of his boyish moods that day —or he just hated to give up, which is his ordinary mood. He had with him the good piece of manila rope with which he

always armed himself before he went goat chasing. He made a noose on one end of the rope, tied the other end to a tough bush, and then dangled the noose over the kidless doe's horns. After a few trials (for the goat would not stand still), the noose fell in place, and Ainslie pulled. Blatting and kicking, the doe was hoisted up over the edge of the barranca, tied to a near-by *palo santo*, and that was that, except for the knife work.

The other three goats remained on the ledge. We wanted to see how they got off, but night came on, and in the morning they were gone. Had they made a standing high jump back on the cliff or had they jumped down?

Another goat hunt was not so odd, but it was considerably more strenuous. One morning when Ainslie arrived at the water-hole with his goat rope and his goat dog, two goats—a doe and her nearly full-grown buck-kid—were nosing around the piece of roofing that covered the catchment basin. Ainslie spoke to the dog and pointed to the fine young buck. Immediately the dog seized him and hung on. Ainslie stepped up, caught a horn with one hand, passed the rope around both horns with the other, and led the buck, much against the latter's will, to a tree and tied him fast. The doe had run away, of course.

Ainslie did his morning's spring work, filled his water buckets, and prepared to return home. Passing, he glanced at his catch to see how he was doing. Two goats stood under the tree—the doe had returned to chew a cud with her offspring. She was an immense, fat doe with a sleek red hide—she had that mouth-watering look, and at the time we were not well off for fat. Ainslie spoke to the dog again, and she went through her usual routine. Ainslie used half of the buck's rope to tie up the doe. So far, very easy.

In the evening Ainslie returned to the spring to fetch his goats, saying, as he left, that he would probably bring back only the young buck. But when he saw the goats again, he was once more impressed by the fat, succulent condition of both of them. One looked about as good as the other—hard to decide which to take.

To sidestep the answer to the question, Ainslie tied the two goats together, head to head, took the two loose rope-ends in his two ex-cavalryman's hands, turned the animals' heads in the direction of El Corral, and said: "Get along, dogies!"

The dogies got along. They ran at full speed, straight through rocky and smooth, bushy and clear, high ground and low ground, all the long mile from the spring to the home gully. The pair of them were too strong for Ainslie to hold back, but he could keep their heads pointed in the right direction. After they had run a mile they were a bit winded, and Ainslie—though more than a bit winded himself—was able to halt them sufficiently to get them tied to a tree, under which they were content to rest for the night.

Ainslie too was content to rest for the night. He preferred to butcher in the evening, to give the meat an opportunity to cool and air out, but this time morning was soon enough. "I had too fast a race for an old man," he said. "I won't do that again."

Our pig hunting was rare and incidental. We could have got pigs often if we had wanted them badly enough to cross the lava into the mountains where good pigs were plentiful. In our dry area of the island hogs were few, and they lived chiefly on roots and drought-resistant weeds—things that had a strong, unpleasant flavour. The goats must have lived partly on the same plants, but the flavours of the diet, whatever it was, blended better with goat meat than with pork. All the pork we got, whether boar-pig or sow-pig, old pig or young pig, had a definite, strong weed, root, and bark taste. One day Ainslie took the trouble to catch, scald, and clean two suckling pigs—they must have been less than four weeks old—and I roasted them whole over good *aromo* coals. But the dog got most of what should have been excellent suckling roast. Even their mother's milk must have been bitter root juice. One thing that must have made the herbage of the vicinity strong-flavoured was the dry, over-sunny climate in which they grew. The sap was not sufficiently diluted with water.

Dove hunting with us was even more incidental and whimsical than pork hunting. We had no flavour-trouble with their meat —they were good eating when barbecued, or stewed with dumplings or rice—but they cost too much in work and time, like all other fine and rare foods. And we did not like to kill our *palomitas*—they were too attractive alive. In fact, we did not like to kill any of the creatures we did kill. Ainslie was always in a low mood for several hours after he had finished butchering. I guess we were not very good cave-men after all.

I killed the first batch of doves we ate. Some fourteen of them had become habitual hangers-on in El Corral. We loved them and wanted them with us, but they loved to snip and pick among my parsley, tomato, and roquette seedlings. They did not eat the plants nor scratch them up as chickens do, but picked, picked, picked with their inch-long bills in the soft, dearly-watered earth, hunting weed seeds and insects perhaps. And as they picked they dug up the plantlets too and left them to wither in the sun. One day I lost my patience. I cut myself a straight, light stick about five feet long and began aiming at the backs of the birds' little iridescent necks. Twelve of the fourteen fell under my stick. The remaining two flew off, though they returned, looking forlorn and lonely, the next day. I let them live.

Some weeks later Ainslie craved dove stew with dumplings, and he too armed himself with a stick and went dove-killing under the *aromo* trees where he was in the habit of tying our donkeys when they spent their nights at home. Doves flocked by the scores to the heaps of burro dung, to pick, pick, pick as was their everlasting habit. Ainslie's stew appetite was big. He was not content with a dozen birds, but killed thirty.

When he was ready to pick them he was aghast at the work he foresaw, especially since he had been without tobacco for several days and was feeling short-tempered and jittery. With as much fortitude and patience as he could muster, he sat down under a tree and, in his turn, started picking, picking, picking. When the thirty little birds were all naked he had another session of being aghast. Now, thirty little heads to snip off, sixty little feet to cut, thirty little crops to take out, thirty little rear-ends to slit open, thirty little sets of guts to remove, thirty tiny hearts to cut out, thirty tiny, soft livers to carve out with infinite care, thirty tiny gizzards to open and clean. Then, thirty headless, footless, gutless, little carcasses to wash twice in clear, cold sea water. The entire operation of killing and dressing took five hours.

When Ainslie brought the panful of doves into the kitchen, the gizzards were arranged neatly around the mound of birds in a sort of garnishing necklace. They were finger-tip size— blue, maroon, opalescent, and beautiful.

"Those gizzards are pearls of great price," Ainslie said wryly. I understood what he meant.

Fishing was much more profitable sport and much less strain on the emotions. Few people sympathise with a fish or feel sorry for him when he is caught, and we were not among those few. A goat or even a bird looks on his butcher with pleading eyes and makes frightened and protesting noises that tear holes in all but the toughest hides. A fish is glassy-eyed and apparently feels no fear or other emotion. He looks so cold that the warm-blooded are cold-blooded at his passing. Fishing is therefore good for the nerves. When he was upset by other killing, Ainslie went fishing to make his peace with the universe. Sometimes I went with him.

When Ainslie fished he always hoped for grouper—our variety was known as *cabrillo* to the San Diego tuna-fishermen, who also liked to eat this fish, and as *bacalao* to the Ecuadorians, who caught it in quantities and salted and dried it. After Ainslie had explored several spots along the lava ledges and boulders that lined part of the neighbouring shore, he found one deep hole at the edge of a lava flow where he could always catch *cabrillo*.

BABY PELICAN

YOUNG FRIGATE BIRD

Nearly every time he went fishing Ainslie also caught a shark. At first he merely killed the sharks and threw them back into the sea, but after we had been on the island for some months and were beginning to think that a little extra ration of vitamin A would do us no harm, he cut out and saved the livers—which I fried and usually ate by myself. Ainslie could not learn to endure the taste.

Plenty of other fish came to Ainslie's hook too—the very first fish he caught was a trigger fish. I have this note in my diary about it:

"First Ainslie caught a red crab for bait. The crab meat was too soft, and something nibbled it off the hook without danger to the nibbler. Then Ainslie tried a grasshopper, which I caught. Nothing happened. The dog was chasing lizards, and I retrieved one she had bitten and dropped. Ainslie cut off one of the forelegs and put it on his hook. Something bit, and Ainsile pulled up on the rocks a flat, lava-coloured fish, with orange mouth parts, and wearing his eyes near the top of his head. He had no gill-openings at his throat, and instead of scales he had a rough, horny skin something like that of a shark. After we had examined him and decided that we did not know him well enough to eat him, Ainslie cut him up for bait. The next fish on the hook was a long, carp-like thing with buck teeth and a bump on his forehead. Ainslie baited the hook with another lizard leg, waited twenty minutes, but caught nothing more. The tide was beginning to wash over the rocks where we were sitting, which ended that fishing attempt."

After that, whenever Ainslie caught a fish he could not name he called it a "scientific fish" and threw it back in the water. We did not think it wise to eat what we could not recognise— some fish are poisonous, or, at least, make you ill. And we did not trust the Polynesian trick taught us by a tuna-fisherman— cooking a silver coin with a strange fish to find out if he is poisonous: if the coin remains bright, the fish is edible; if it turns black, so will you if you eat the fish.

Another fish story in my diary goes like this:

"Ainslie went fishing again out on his favourite rocks to the west. After some time he caught a small sea iguana and baited his hook with pieces of iguana flesh. Within five

F

minutes he had caught two four-pound *cabrillos*. He could have caught more, but two were enough for our household, including the dog and chickens. We had all we could eat of fried fish for dinner and there was plenty of cold fish left over for my breakfast. Ainslie will not eat fish for breakfast, certainly when it is left over and cold."

Gentle sport, fishing.

Ainslie did not like lobster fishing, and I never tried it. Catching lobsters without a trap involved too much scrambling over slippery, tide-washed rocks, too much wading up to your chin and even swimming, too much sticking your head under salt water, and too much groping among spiny carapaces and who knows what else that might be lurking in the dark, rocky crevices. Lobster was not worth all this trouble to us, and after trying it a time or two just for the experience Ainslie said: "Not for me," and went back to grouper and shark fishing. Less sport perhaps, but more pleasure and relaxation, and also less sea water to wash out of the hair and ears afterward.

Among the rocks at low tide we sometimes searched for *ganchas al mar*, as the Ecuadorians call a species of chiton found on some of the Galápagos shores, but we never found any— perhaps we did not know just where to look. The Ecuadorians chop up the flesh, cure it a few hours in lemon juice, and serve it well-seasoned as a first course to "open the appetite" or in a salad with raw onions and other vegetables. The *ganchas* are a bit tough to chew, but appetising nevertheless.

On occasion, while Ainslie manœuvred for sharks and groupers and "scientific fish," I found sport in making a collection of "finds"; the case of the broken pottery had got me started. Whatever I found, if it was not the sort of thing that occurred on the island naturally, was exciting to me—and to Ainslie—for it involved an explanation or at least an imaginary answer to the question: "How did this thing get here?" Some items were not difficult to account for. We never could explain the presence of others. And even when my finds were expected or indigenous, like shells, goat bones, or plants, if they were beautiful or odd they gave us pleasure and something to wonder about.

Hopping and scrambling among the rocks, often on all fours, and kicking at stones and shells along the beaches, I collected in the course of several fishing trips a rather formidable miscellany, which I kept in what I called my "museum"—the top of the corral wall behind the house. Ten pieces of beautiful sun-bleached coral—white or pink-and-white—these specimens I had chosen for perfection of form, for I could have had ten million unselected pieces. Twenty different species of shells—here again I could have had ten million individuals though not that many species. A dozen assorted seal bones, mostly shoulder blades because of their interesting shape. One small mayonnaise jar, "Best Foods" brand, with a couple of spoonfuls of mayonnaise still in it. Two bottles, one brown, one green. Two coffee cans, Maxwell House and Schilling's. A weathered Sunkist orange crate. A new, red-painted Coca-Cola crate. One piece of driftwood—Ainslie said it was California redwood. Twenty pebbles.

On our land excursions I picked up other treasures: In addition to the coarse, red stuff that was so abundant, I found a few other pieces of finer red clay, glazed, and decorated with a red-and-green flower design, and the larger half of a pitcher made of fine grey clay, also glazed, and decorated with a brown, spotted design. Several bits of chinaware, plain white or flower adorned. Two enamel-ware cups. One rusted chamber pot. One enamel-ware kettle, without a bottom. One square glass bottle, sun-coloured to a nice violet shade. Two small aluminium boxes, with the tops cut off. Half of an old sword-blade. Two rusty knife-blades. One perfectly good metal coat-hanger. Six feet of chicken fence. Several pieces of barb-wire. Six machine-gun cartridges. Dozens of old nails, some handmade. One fountain-pen cap.

These are not quite all, but they give the picture. I doubt that anyone else ever made such a collection, unless it were a Colorado trade rat. In time I added to it three goat skulls, complete with horns, and two burro skulls that grinned with long teeth. I hoped to get paint some time to decorate them into devil-masks.

Perhaps—though I don't find it easy to confess the weakness—I was secretly hoping to find some more valuable treasure. But diligently as I searched, I found no pieces of eight, no doubloons, no gold bracelets, no diamond and emerald necklaces. I did not even find a thin United States dime, though I did find one Ecuadorian *dos reales* piece, which I may have dropped myself. Our pirates had hidden their treasure well, or else they had spent it all in Panama and other treasure-gobbling places—as any sensible pirate would have done.

I also hunted for eggs—and now you probably imagine me digging the beaches for turtle eggs or robbing doves' nests. Wrong. I hunted only for hens' eggs—familiar, domestic hens' produce. Or perhaps I did not hunt eggs, but tried to make hunting them unnecessary. Whatever the definition, the activity was sometimes amusing.

We had brought three hens from San Cristóbal, and we had named them Yellow Hen, Red Hen, and Grey Hen. Each of these hens had a third interest in a rooster—a big, clumsy, feather-legged lummox, whom I called Pegasus. Ainslie called him "Feather-legged This and That." Pegasus needs to be mentioned in connection with the egg-hunting business for he took an active part in it.

All the hens laid about equally well, and followed the usual tropical hen routine—two weeks of laying, but missing a few days so that each managed only ten or twelve eggs in that period, followed by two weeks of sitting fever and rest. Sometimes, in one manner or another, the fever period could be shortened, but the eggless days still remained unchanged in number. To keep up this "two weeks by two weeks" routine required some human interference—otherwise the hens would have laid one clutch of eggs and spent the following three months raising a family. I forced them into a system of birth control, for Ainslie and I needed eggs in our diet and we were not yet ready to handle more chickens.

Each hen had her own personal whims and preferences as to where she wanted to lay and how she wanted to go about it. Pegasus adapted himself to all the caprices of his harem and did everything he could to help and encourage. I also adapted myself.

Our chickens roamed loose over the flat and the canyon and spent their nights in a *muyuyu* tree near the beach. They were not permitted to enter El Corral, which they took as a hardship, for on San Cristóbal they had been tolerated in any house they cared to visit. Yellow Hen had been a special pet—she had roosted on the footboard of her mistress's bed and, if I understood the story correctly, laid her eggs in her mistress's lap.

So when Yellow Hen, who was always first in everything, began looking for a place to lay, she came straight into the house. Pegasus came with her, giving advice and encouragement in a low, guttural voice. Since Ainslie was not at home to object to the proceedings, and I could see that important business was in the wind, I played deaf and dumb, but kept my eyes open. I had plans of my own.

Pegasus scratched and wallowed in the corner behind my bed, talking to his hen the while, as if saying: "Just leave it all to me, dear. I'll soon have a cosy little place for you to lay your egg in. You don't need to worry your pretty little head at all."

But Yellow Hen was not convinced. She left the rooster to his scratching and wallowing, and moved away, singing softly to herself. She peered into corners and boxes and dark spots, raising her head now and then to see if she was being observed. She stopped beside a gunny sack nearly full of crushed newspapers—papers which had been used for packing dishes and tools and which I had saved for whatever it might be good for. Yellow Hen hopped up on the sack, scratched and picked at the papers hopefully, then burrowed into them, rear-end first, until only her bill was visible.

I waited a few minutes until she was well settled, then sneaked up behind her, snatched her up and clapped her under a box. The hen safe, I chased the rooster all the way to Pirate Flat. I could not stomach his self-important attitude. By the time he returned to the canyon he had forgotten the egg business and went to dally with his other two hens under the roosting *muyuyu*.

An hour later I lifted the box and found that the hen had accomplished her intention. I tossed her over the corral wall, for she was drowsy and reluctant to move, picked up the egg, and stirred it into my pancake batter. The next day Yellow Hen returned to the sack of papers, and I repeated the routine of catching and boxing her—and so on for twelve days.

The day after she had laid her twelfth egg Yellow Hen came into the kitchen, puffed up into a ball of feathers standing on end, and clucking like an outboard motor. She wanted to get into the sack or the box or any quiet place and just sit. If she could find an egg to sit on, very good—but she would be content with a white stone or the bleached, discarded shell of a hermit crab, or nothing at all. Sitting was the important thing. Knowing that there would be no egg that day, I tried to shoo her out, but she refused to be shooed. She retreated a few steps, racing her motor, turned, and tried to duck between my legs to reach the house. I caught her, tied a string to her leg, and tethered her to a limb of the roosting tree—which was far enough away so that I could not hear her irritating motor running—in such a way that she could not squat down. Tied up this way

—day and night, without any rations except water—she was over her fever in three days.

When Yellow Hen's next egg-laying period came, she was accustomed to being handled by me, and I caught her without preliminaries or ceremony, when she came into El Corral to look for a nest, and put her under her box.   Soon she was so well trained that I was saved even the heavy work of catching.   She came to the gate of El Corral, squawked softly, and looked at me expectantly.   I stooped and held out my hands.   Yellow Hen walked into them.

I was never able to come to similar, cosy terms with the Red and the Grey.   They had been brought up in a different household.

Red Hen was independent.   She seldom consorted with the other chickens, but preferred to go off grasshopper hunting to the east if the others went west.   She roosted on a limb by herself, higher up than the other hens.   She was snooty.

About her egg-laying she was casual, and yet in a way sophisticated.   At nest-hunting time she did not want the rooster with her, which made Pegasus look puzzled and hurt.   If he went in one direction she went in another, or if he followed her, she quit searching and climbed up on her daytime roost and acted as if she had no cares whatever.   When the rooster had forgotten about her or become discouraged, she came down and resumed her casual searching.   She looked into the fork of a tree, behind a rock, up at a gunny sack hung on a limb—cawing absent-mindedly, and taking time now and then to catch and eat a lizard. I tried to keep my eye on her to see where she finally chose to stop—this was difficult, for she sometimes searched for hours— but she had a way of disappearing, right out of my eye as it were. Yet, when she finally laid her egg, it would be in the most obvious place possible—under her own roosting limb, under a thin bush beside the corral gate, or in a shady spot on the path which we used many times a day travelling from El Corral to the seashore.

Grey Hen was a problem.   She was nervous and capricious and very, very finicky.   She drove Pegasus frantic with her specifications, demands and complaints when those two went nest-hunting.   With endless patience and good nature he did his utmost, but at last she told him he never would learn and bid him be off to other work—if, indeed, he had other work.   She would find just what she wanted by herself, without any muddling, heavy-footed interference from him.

"But, my one and only," said the tired and puzzled Pegasus, "that red-covered bed there in the house is the perfect place, and you know I showed you that—even tried sitting on it to make sure it was soft enough.   You laid on a worse bed before."

"And you forget, *tonto*—when don't you forget?—that the bed was in Señora Angelita's house."

"This house is as good as Señora Angelita's, and the bed is better.   I don't understand your objection, *chiquita*."

"Who said you understood?   When have you understood anything?   This house with the shiny, tin roof belongs to that *gringa* in the short, red pants—Señora Angelita wore a blue dress remember?   I don't trust these *gringa norteamericanas*.   How do I know she won't steal my eggs and eat all of them?   Señora Angelita always left me at least six to *sacar pollitos*.   And I can't even sneak under her bed without her spying on me.   If I could only get there without being seen, she might not be able to find my egg in that dark corner with those black sun-blinkers she wears.   The only other half-way possible place is under that big thorn bush—and the *cholos*, dogs, and pigs will find my eggs there."

"There are no *cholos* on Santiago, the pigs are far away, and the dog is always so full of goat meat that she won't bother your eggs.   You are not on San Cristóbal now, my pretty."

"Your pretty, indeed!   You might at least say 'my prettiest" you three-timing Don Juan.   And I wish I were back at Puerto Chico."

"But, my very prettiest, three-timing is small-timing, as any cock at Puerto Chico would tell you, if you were there now. Why, El Rojo was a regular twelve-timer, and no one ever threw that in his bill.   He was an honoured and respected *padre de muchas familias.*   And speaking of Puerto Chico, there was that plump, white *pollita* at Señora Carmelita's house, and though I suppose I should not mention it—she and I—but there, *querida*, you are worth two of her.   Now what about that nest, chicken?"

"Don't you chicken me!   And get out of my sight before I peck your roving eyes out—you and your white *pollita!*   I've just got to get this egg laid—do you think I can hold it all day? You drive me so frantic that I'll probably have no egg at all tomorrow.   Now, get, get, get!"

"But, baby, don't you want me to stay with you to comfort you?   That egg is my egg too, you know."

"My egg, he says.   Where do you get that stuff?   I've laid eggs before, and many times—but, of course, those were *huevos de viento* and I never got any *pollitos* out of them.   Goody—there goes the *gringa* to the beach.   Maybe now I can sneak under the bed.   But you stay away from me.   You make altogether too much noise with your big feet, and you know how furious she gets when she finds us in the house—especially you."

When I came back from the beach, where I had gone to wash weed seeds, pebbles, and *tierra santa del Ecuador* out of a panful of lentils, I saw a red spot under Ainslie's bed—Grey Hen's comb it was.   I made as if I had not seen her, then stole quietly behind the house, came like a ghost around the corner, and snatched her up before she knew what was happening.   She squawked and struggled as I tied a long stout string to her leg.   I had some real plans for Grey Hen.   I was going to give her a house of her own to lay in, thinking that she, of all the hens, would appreciate a quiet, secluded spot most.

I tied Grey Hen to a tree and went out to build a nest-house. At the side of the canyon, in the shade of a thorn bush, was a pile of rocks.   I arranged these to form three walls—only two feet high—of a yard-square shelter.   Quickly I cut thorn-bush limbs for a thatch, found a large slab of tufa for a door, and

made a perfect nest of crushed and torn newspapers. Then I
fetched the hen, tied the loose end of her string to a heavy rock,
poked her into the house, and closed the door.

There was a moment of silence. Then the hen set up a
terrific squawking and struggled to come out through the thorn-
bush roof. Finding herself tied fast, she went into hysterics, and
got herself and the string hopelessly tangled with the thorn-bush
limbs. Pegasus heard her squawking and came galloping up

like a Percheron stallion—adding his raucous "Cawk, cawk,
cawk" to the cacophony. The other two hens heard and started
cackling. The dog heard and started barking.

"Heavens and all other places!" I thought. "There is an
egg somewhere in this mess and medley! What will happen to
it? And at this rate, Grey Hen will be shocked into permanent
sterility."

I threw aside the thorn limbs that were not entangled with
the hen, and cut the string close to her leg. Grey Hen flew,
not ran, the twenty yards to the roosting tree, climbed to the
highest limb, squawking hideously the while. The dog and the
other chickens ran after her to the foot of the tree, each screaming
riot in his own language.

Two hours passed before Grey Hen was calm enough to remember that she had an egg to lay. This time she did not come into El Corral and detoured widely around the horror spot of the nest-house. She walked warily up the little hill behind El Corral, where there was an incredibly thick and low-grown clump of thorn bushes. I did not dare to follow her for fear she would throw another fit. Several hours later, toward evening, I went to investigate. I looked all around the bushes and under them wherever I could see the tiniest opening, but I could find no egg though I did find an old-fashioned, hand-made wine bottle.

I did not give up hope, however, for it seemed that the hen must have laid under the bush somewhere—there was no other cover near. Finding a place where the limbs hung as high as a foot above the rocky ground, I flattened down on my front elevation and started crawling under, forgetting for the time about scorpions and centipedes—I was too busy evading thorns to remember them. And sure enough, three yards from daylight, was a white egg, carefully cupped in a perfect nest of dry thorns.

Knowing my hen now a little better, I left the egg until she should have laid another. I was afraid she would leave this nest and find a more distant and even more difficult one if I left the nest eggless. It seems that hens can count up to one—or at least that is as far as they can remember from today until tomorrow.

For the next laying period Grey Hen found another thorn bush. She always laid under thorn bushes—at least six different ones—except once. That time Ainslie and I had been absent from El Corral all day, and Grey Hen had laid in just the spot she would always have chosen if she could have been absolutely free and unmolested. That day her large, white egg rested comfortably in the middle of Ainslie's bed.

VIII. A PANCAKE IS A PANCAKE IS NOT
A PANCAKE

I have made two hundred different kinds of pancakes. Gross
exaggeration? No. The number may even exceed two hundred
if I count all the little variations, such as the different kinds of
fat used in cooking them—and I don't have to count such
extremely minor items as the various kinds of griddles and stoves
and fireplaces I have used. During my years in the Galápagos
I doubt if I ever followed exactly the same recipe more than
twice, yet almost every day I made pancakes in some form.
Even hash sometimes ended as a pancake.

I had an early start in pancakes about the age of seven.
Pancakes were the first things I learned to cook. My very
earliest variety was conventional—the usual mixture of white
flour, sour milk, soda, and salt cooked with lard in a cast-iron
griddle. A second variety was soon born, for I don't like to
repeat myself—I added a good half-cup of sugar one morning,
prompted by my childish craving for sweets. The result suited
me, but mother was not pleased. The sweet milk and baking
powder recipe came next, embellished by the addition of an egg
and a couple of tablespoons of melted butter.

By the time I was ten, I had learned to make several of
the more exotic varieties. Among others, there was the blood
pancake and the Scandinavian version of the milk pancake—
which is not cooked in a griddle on the stove but baked in
the oven.

The first of these is mixed and cooked just like the ordinary
baking powder flapjack, except that instead of milk fresh blood
is used. Beef, hog, or sheep blood will do—even chicken blood,
if you can get enough of it. The result is a rich, mahogany
brown in colour and most flavourful and satisfying to eat—with
butter or bacon fat only, no sugar or syrup. I heartily recommend blood pancakes even to modern *gringos*, who, for all their
vaunted knowledge of good food, have little experience with
really savoury dishes.

The oven pancake is special. To make it in the orthodox
manner, you must have somewhere in the vicinity a newborn

calf less than four days old. The presence of that newcomer means that his mother is giving milk which is thick and yellow. You mix the conventional batter with this unconventional liquid, beating thoroughly—and you may omit the leavening. Then you pour a very thin sheet of the batter in a bread pan or a cookie sheet and bake it in a hot oven about ten minutes. It comes out a luscious brown and puffed up with heated air— though, on cooling, it flattens down again. (This batter could be baked in muffin tins, but then it would result in a batch of pop-overs.) For serving, several of these sheets are stacked like a layer cake, with butter and sugar in between, cut into squares or wedges, and brought to the table hot. They will do for dessert or make a complete meal. To me they taste best with cold milk, though many prefer them with coffee. A similar result could probably be obtained by mixing a batter with ordinary sweet milk and eggs, but I can't say for sure. I never tried that variation—which shows that I still have something to learn about pancake making.

However, not until I came to the Galápagos did I realise just how versatile pancakes are and how much adventure there is in eating them. In the islands I learned fast, because usually the ingredients I could get were not those that cook books ask for. We grow inventive when our accustomed groove is absent.

The first pancakes I made in the Galápagos—this happened in May, 1937, on the second day of our acquaintance with Santiago—were somewhat like the first ones I learned to make at home, though with variations my mother would not have approved. I had no prepared salt handy, so I used part sea water for mixing the batter, and powdered milk and fresh water instead of whole milk, for I had no whole milk either. I baked those cakes with pure olive oil over a smoky "squaw-wood" fire burning in a niche of lava rocks. A few weeks afterward, when my powdered milk and baking powder were gone, I simply omitted the one and substituted baking soda and a few drops of acetic acid for leavening. To get the porportions right cost me some close calculating, observant experience, and lucky guessing. Also a few dismal failures, which had to be eaten, anyway.

Then, as the wheat flour grew short and finally disappeared, I began to mix the batter with corn or rice flour or both, ground in a little handmill. And when I had it—which was nearly always during our subsequent years on Floreana Island—I used lemon juice to supply the acid necessary with bicarbonate of soda. If I had no soda, what then? Either I made the cakes without leavening, or I used clean, white ashes.   Pancake making is an adventurous business, you see, and you can make them with almost anything.

On Floreana, where we had an orchard and a garden, our pancakes could really go to town—or take to the woods, if you prefer that expression.   For variety and flavour and bulk, whenever those considerations moved me—or if I had to, out of plain, everyday necessity—I included in the batter grated raw potatoes, either sweet or white, grated yuca (manioc) or otoy (taro), or fine diced bananas—any of five varieties of bananas. In my opinion, white potatoes or the limeño variety of bananas made the best mixtures.

There was also the pancake made entirely without grain flour of any kind.   These, in my al fresco kitchen, were concocted of white or sweet potatoes—several kinds of sweet potatoes, which we are in the habit of calling *camotes*—yuca, otoy, squash, or dominico bananas.   My methods of preparation varied with mood and necessity—the ingredients could first be boiled or baked, then mashed and seasoned and mixed with an egg or two, if I had eggs, or the roots or fruits could be grated fine, formed into flat cakes, and baked or fried like any other pancakes.   Sometimes I flavoured the mashed sweet potato cakes with orange juice or nutmeg.   Nutmeg, cloves, or cinnamon— or all three—did nice things to the squash.

The strictly corn pancake was again another thing—or several other things.   Often these were a very simple mixture of hand-ground corn meal, water, salt, and no leavening.   The corn used was not always the same—I made meal of hard yellow corn, hard white corn, or soft yellow corn, the Ecuadorian *serrano* variety, that is.   Sometimes I added grated onion to the corn cake batter—a United States negro innovation—and then we ate the so-called "Louisiana Hush-puppies."   Now and then the corn was first made into hominy, then pounded or ground to a paste, formed into thin cakes, and baked without grease—which gave us Mexican *tortillas*.   Still another good trick was mixing the corn meal with soup stock or gravy, or adding bits of meat, either fat or lean.   In mixing corn meal cakes, the liquid has to be boiling hot, or the batter will not be sticky enough to hold together—unless, of course, you add eggs.

If you are a Westerner of the older generation, you have heard of bean pancakes.   Also, very likely, you have eaten them. Ainslie introduced me to them, and he got the recipe from his mother, the daughter of a 'Forty-niner. She learned to make them as a small girl when she crossed the continent in a covered wagon. The method is simple. Just take some beans that have been cooked rather dry. Mash them fine. Season. Pat into cakes and fry. I said fry and I stick to it. 'Forty-niners fried everything—usually in bacon fat. You can travel a long way on a good breakfast of bean cakes and feel equal to combating whatever storms, floods, slides, or wild Indians might come along.

The same trick can be played on cooked peas, lentils, *garbanzos* (chick-peas), spaghetti, macaroni, corn meal mush, rice mush, or hash—anything not too dry, yet dry enough to stick together. After all, why be stuffy and always follow what the books say? Some person, much like yourself, invented the recipes and wrote the book—it did not fall in a blaze of miraculous light from heaven. Invent something of your own— especially if you just have to, in order to keep on eating.

Stuffiness reminds me—of stuffed pancakes. These too are of many kinds—as to the cake itself and the filling. I received a few samples from our Ecuadorian friends; others Ainslie and I invented. Take any of the pre-cooked pancake mixtures— *camote* and squash are preferred by our friends in Guayaquil and Puerto Chico—make a thin cake, spread it with finely chopped, cooked meat, season with discretion or bold imagination, put another thin cake on top, and bake slowly on both sides. Or stuff with chopped vegetables—peppers and onions, for example —or with dry fruits, seasoning and flavouring according to your taste and mood. Or you may mix all three—meat, vegetables and fruit.

Now, what to use for cooking fat? All the usual ones—if you have them—or beef fat, goat fat, chicken fat, tortoise fat, or no fat at all, if you have that kind of griddle. I have tried donkey fat too, but I do not recommend it. I have heard of using fish oil, sea turtle oil, and seal oil, though the flavours of these would probably not combine well with anything but fish pancakes. Oh, yes, I have made fish pancakes—and you can invent a few recipes for them yourself, if you are interested.

Still one more source of variation—what shall we use as a spread for our cakes—syrup, sugar, butter, jam, jelly, fruit sauce, bacon fat, meat drippings, cream, gravy, and are there still a few other things? Indeed there are. Soups and *purées* of any kind—though with some respect to the individuality of the cakes —white sauce, cheese sauce, *salsa ranchera*—which is the Mexican version of chili sauce—catsup, peanut butter, mustard, tomato sauce, or whatever you happen to think of and your palate will accept. Some of the Conways' favourite spreads are—when they can get them—hot marrow fat, orange syrup, pineapple syrup, naranjilla jam, and cream and sugar. But do use a little discretion—not all spreads will go with all cakes, and some cakes are best with no spread at all. The stuffed cakes, especially, are complete in themselves.

I have not yet emptied my mind of all my pancake ideas, but I have exhibited enough of them to show what sort of cooking I did at the sandstone fireplace in El Corral.

Pancake time in El Corral was usually around noon. Ainslie hardly ever takes anything but coffee in the morning, at least three cupfuls of it, and it was not worth the effort to cook anything more for myself. I could take a few crackers—Ecuadorian *galletas*—with my coffee, or perhaps a couple of cold pancakes or a biscuit left over from the previous day. Toast would have suited me much better, or crisp, crusty French rolls. That I knew very well; but merely knowing this did me no good.

Ordinarily I baked thirty average-sized cakes every day—the wheat flour, soda, citric or acetic acid, and water variety, with an egg or two added. During the first weeks I had milk powder, and now and then for the variety I craved, I used part rice flour or cooked rice instead of all wheat flour. I enriched the batter with a tablespoonful or two of oil while the oil lasted, and put in a heaping tablespoonful of sugar to encourage the cakes to brown better. These I baked in a very wide Ecuadorian frying pan, hand-hammered out of a sheet of iron—the sheet obtained by opening up and flattening an old gasoline drum. Such hand-hammered utensils are much commoner and cheaper in Eucador than factory-made articles, which are imported. As long as I had it, I used the Argentine "lard" we had purchased in Guayaquil after having waited several half-days in the rationing office for a permit. This so-called lard was probably a mixture of beef or goat fat and whale oil—certainly it was not lard as we knew it. When that was gone, I greased the pan with goat fat, which is very much like beef fat in texture and flavour.

On days when pancakes seemed unbearable to me—Ainslie as a good Western mountaineer could eat them every morning —I made biscuits, which were a sort of pancake, too, for I baked them over the coals in a heavy aluminium frying pan, covered with a sheet of metal cut for the purpose and heaped with coals and ashes. The biscuits were made as nearly according to the standard pattern as my resources would permit—I used water instead of milk and sometimes added an egg and a little sugar, which turned them into scones. I never rolled out my biscuit dough or cut it with the usual round cutter—I merely flattened it down into the pan with my hands and cut it into wedges with a knife before baking. One panful was enough for two days—on the second morning I put the pan of biscuits on the coals and ashes to reheat.

One day Ainslie told me how his mother used to make "dough-gods," though he was not able to explain why they were so oddly named. Dough-gods are fruit biscuits, but fried in deep fat they are more like unsweetened dough-nuts. To keep them in the class of biscuits they should be cooked slowly in a well-greased frying pan until they have a brown crust at the bottom, then turned to brown on the other side. Dough-gods were another 'Forty-niner delicacy, Ainslie said. I made them several times, though for me they were anything but delicate. However, I had to admit that for providing the energy and the internal fortitude necessary to fight murderous Indians they had their value.

We ate our pancakes with syrup I made of plain or caramelised sugar and flavoured with nutmeg, cloves, or cinnamon. For the biscuits I made peanut butter—I had to roast and grind my own peanuts—or we spread them with hot goat fat and a sprinkling of salt. A few times I attempted preserves of wild ground cherries and home-grown water-melon rind. We eked out our simple noon meal with black coffee and such meat as we happened to have—our favourite breakfast meat dish was a mixed fry of goat liver, kidneys, brains, and chops. Sometimes Ainslie accepted a plateful of beans with his pancakes—another taste he had acquired from his pioneer parents—and I ate cold fish, for such had been the habit of my ancestors.

For dinner I had to get away from pancakes and turn to my other specialty, the meat dish. In six cases out of seven, my meat dish was of ancient and honoured lineage, for once it had been served up on bloody altars to blood-thirsty gods and had been avidly consumed by them in a burst of flame and smoke. Indeed, Jehovah provided a horned goat for himself on at least one terrible occasion.

A certain kid which the dog unfortunately caught one day before Ainslie could direct her to other game was a doubly qualified candidate for sacrificial offering. He must have fed on *palo santo* leaves, though usually goats do not eat them, for his flesh which I broiled carefully over a bed of coals, was highly seasoned with *palo santo*—the name means "holy tree." We would have been willing to place that succulent-looking kid on the altar of any god who wanted him.

Although we had had nothing to say about what animals should be provided for us on Santiago, we could not have chosen better if we had given the order ourselves.   The little animals can live almost anywhere on almost anything, they multiply fast, are easy to catch, grow to just the right size for conditions where fresh meat cannot be kept fresh for more than two or three days, and the meat is of good flavour and can be prepared for eating in many ways.   It was really fortunate for us that Captain Porter had had the misfortune to lose his milch goats on Santiago Island.

Our goat-cooking mornings were busy mornings and they began early.   At the crack of dawn Ainslie got up, pulled on his shoes and shorts, dashed a little water on his face, and passed a comb through his hair.   He took off immediately for the tree where he had hung his butchered and dressed goat for the night. He brought it to El Corral, hung it on a *muyuyu* limb, and started cutting it in pieces for the kettles, trimming out the fat first.

In the meantime I had made a fire and put the coffee kettle on.   When the coffee was done, and I had poured out a cupful for each of us, I began cutting up the fat into a Dutch oven for trying out.   I watched the frying tallow carefully so that the *chicharrones* (cracklings) would brown and crisp nicely but not burn, for they were good eating with pancakes or mixed into *frijoles refritos*—a Mexican version of fried beans.   When the fat was rendered, I took out the *chicharrones*, and poured it into a powdered milk can, which had the advantage of a good lid.

By this time Ainslie had dug out the meat grinder and was making hamburger—or was it sausage?   He mixed plenty of salt, pepper, minced garlic, and sage or allspice into the ground meat, which I formed into flat cakes and fried immediately.   The grinding finished, Ainslie put as much of the ribs and the vertebrae into the soup kettle as it would hold, cut some of the loin muscle and one of the hams into roasting pieces, and made the shoulder meat and the other ham into strips for drying or smoking.   The brains, kidneys, some of the liver, and a dozen chops he set aside in a pan.

On an ordinary morning we might have been hungry by this time, but so much odour of frying fat and meat filled our nostrils that eating was something to be shunned.   Ainslie had drunk his three or four cups of coffee while he worked, and I went on with my cooking—though, heaven knows, I would rather have left El Corral for a place where the air was not so pleasant to the nostrils of Jove or Jehovah.

First I browned the pieces for the pot roast, then added seasonings and slivers of garlic, and clapped them under the heavy cover of the roaster. I added no water, for the meat was juicy, and I cooked it slowly until it was no longer rare but still not tender. Then I put the roaster in a cool, shady spot, leaving the cover on, to wait until the following day for further cooking. Then I seasoned the soup meat and boiled it only long enough to keep until the next day. The first day's eating —and part of the second day's—would be hamburgers, cold or warmed over, and the mixed fry, which was waiting to be cooked last so that it would be hot for breakfast.

In the afternoon, when the cooking was finished, I hung the strips, which Ainslie had cut for curing, over a slow, smoky fire of thorn wood—this wood had been recommended to us by one of the Norwegian pioneers of Santa Cruz. I caught the thin pieces of meat on wire hooks Ainslie had made for the purpose, hung the hooks on a coat-hanger I had found, and the hanger, in its turn, on an overhanging *muyuyu* limb. The flank pieces and other scraps destined for the dog I draped over the limbs of a dead and fallen *aromo* a short distance up the canyon.

On the second day of goat cooking I finished the roast and made the soup. I had various things to add to the soup—onions and potatoes during the first few months, garlic, rice, five different kinds of beans, *garbanzos*, lentils, and ground peanuts. The island provided few additions too—grass, *aromo*, and mint leaves, which I chopped very fine and used with discretion. Later, with the help of my own garden, I had chopped cucumber, pumpkin, water-melon, parsley, and *roquette* leaves. I did not always bother to tell Ainslie what the green stuff was—and he seldom looked away often enough from his dinner-time book to notice and ask.

The soup and the pot roast were re-cooked on at least two days, and by that time they had been eaten up by us, the dog, and the chickens. Sometimes I used the final left-overs for hash or fried them with beans or *garbanzos*. The smoked meat was good eaten uncooked in little between-meal snacks or made into hash with potatoes or *garbanzos*.

While we were waiting in Guayaquil for the *Calderón* to make her island trip, Ainslie had envisioned fun on Santiago with a barbecue outfit, as he called it. Though I did not fancy myself

as a barbecue cook and gave Ainslie no encouragement, he kept
on envisioning, until nothing could keep him from going to a
cholo blacksmith and ordering the outfit made to specifications.
It was not easy to make the *cholo* understand something outside
his experience, but Ainslie patiently drew pictures and described
in detail. The outfit turned out to be a variety of iron bars—
some plain, others flat with saw-tooth edges, and one long one
with a double angle at both ends. These, when properly
assembled, made a spit on which a whole goat could be impaled
and which could be turned with a cranking action on a sturdy,
fireproof frame.

This invention worked exactly as Ainslie had meant it to
work. The only way our barbecuing differed from Ainslie's
dream of it was that it never happened. Or rather, it did
happen, but on that occasion the Conways were not the cooks.

The eating of fish and the few dinners which featured doves
or lobster came between goats, as it were, when Ainslie was fed
up with butchering or when we craved a little change. My fish
cooking was simple—frying, broiling, or steaming. The doves
made soup with rice, stew with dumplings, or were fried or
broiled. The lobster, of course, had to be boiled alive first
—I used sea water—then removed from the shell, cut into pieces,
and, in our household, seasoned with salt, pepper, garlic, vinegar,
and olive oil. We knew something about lobster with mayonnaise and lobster thermidor, but our ingredients stopped short of
these fancy preparations.

Though meat and fish were so abundant, there were days
when we made our dinner of beans and rice, in the Latin-
American poor man's manner, for we tired of animal food in
hot weather. We could put some variety into our bean cooking
too, for we had many kinds of beans and knew many ways of
preparing them—Ainslie, of all persons, should have been an
expert on beans. *Purée* or soup of the Andean *habas*—Ainslie
called them horse-beans—was excellent, though there was one
drawback to making it—the beans had to be divested of their
tough, thick hides before they could be used.

I cooked rice as the Latin-Americans do, using only as much
water as the grains will absorb in cooking—which is two cupfuls
to one cupful of washed rice. Usually I cooked enough one day
to last also for the next—there are many good ways of warming
rice over. My favourite method was to spread the cooked rice
on the bottom of a heavy, generously greased frying pan, adding
a little salt, covering tightly, and letting the pan stand on rather

low heat for about half an hour. The rice would then have a crunchy, brown crust at the bottom and be fluffy all the rest of the way. When I had eggs to spare, I mixed the rice with egg and dropped the mixture by spoonfuls into the frying pan— perhaps I had another pancake there. Rice cakes could also be made by mixing the cooked rice with a plain batter of flour and water and frying. Often I dropped spoonfuls of the flour or egg mixture of rice into boiling soup—a little chopped, cooked meat was good in these.

It is scarcely possible these days to forget about vitamins, even on a desert island, and since our island was not the sort of paradise where wild fruits fall into your open mouth every time you happen to be snoring in the shade of a tree, we had to give our vitamins more than a little thought. We knew we were getting certain kinds of vitamins in sufficient quantities from the fresh meat and fish we ate—though our manner of cooking and re-cooking may have wasted some of these. Remained at least A and C to think of—they are usually obtained from fresh fruits and vegetables—though I believe that I was literally saturated with vitamin A after each time I ate a whole shark liver.

You already know that I used some of the island's native greenery in soup. We had been told that it is safe to eat whatever leaves and fruit domestic animals—or even wild animals— relish, and our own common sense and observation repeated it. Goats, donkeys, and chickens, as well as wild birds and insects, were fond of *aromo* leaves. After I had tried chewing a few *aromo* leaves myself and found them rather tasteless and apparently harmless, I would wash and chop a half-cupful of them for the gallon or two of soup I had in the making. Another leaf I tested and used in the same way belonged to a shrub of the mint family—at any rate, the square stem and the aroma of the plant led me to believe that it was one of the mints. *Muyuyu* leaves and blossoms proved edible too, but until new foliage appeared in February, the leaves were too tough and hard to be palatable. With the advent of the heavier rains late in January, there was plenty of grass, though not all of it was considered edible by the donkeys and chickens. We watched these animals at their grazing, sampled a few stems, and found a couple of varieties that were edible for the Conways also.

Our favourite way to get vitamins from grass was to pick a nice, fresh bunch of it—all we could get into our mouths comfortably—and chew it as a cow chews her cud. As we chewed we kept on swallowing the juice with our saliva, and when all the flavour was gone from the grass we spat it out and picked another cud. Each of us made a point of chewing four cuds a day, and, if we felt like it—especially when cigarettes or other smokables were few or absent—we chewed oftener.

"Have you had your grass today?" we would remind each other, or "Won't you come and chew a cud with me?"

Some distance inland from the beaches grew a dark-green semi-climber, which the Ecuadorians call *monte salada*—it can be translated as "salty bush." This was a great favourite with goats —every bush we found was picked clean of leaves and young shoots from the ground up as far as a grown goat can reach by standing on his two hind legs like a man. We chewed some of these leaves, too, and I considered them as possible soup ingredients, but they had an extremely strong, salty flavour and rough texture, so we let the goats keep all of that delicacy—at least until other edible greens were not to be had.

The thorn bush, which was always as green as mangrove though it had no true leaves except in the rainy season—and then very few, bore quantities of small reddish-black berries, which had a pit something like that of a cherry and were of a sweetish but insipid taste. Doves and finches were fond of them —sometimes the crops of the doves we killed were filled with thorn berries. They were too small for Ainslie to bother with— or perhaps he did not care to compete with the birds—but I often picked a handful or two and ate them with some satisfaction. They seemed to provide, in a small way, the fruity flavours I was always craving.

The *muyuyus* put on a few berries too, so did the *palos santos*, *chalas*, and the few remaining specimens of the shrubbery that had died during the dry years. We did not try eating the *palo santo* berries—to us, everything connected with *palos santos* was strictly for smelling, not eating—and there was not enough of the others for even a few families of finches.

A certain kind of salt-savoury seaweed was thrown up on the beach now and then, and we always picked this up, dried it, and ate it, bit by bit, without cooking. There were other sea-weeds among the rocks within reach at low tide, and the sea iguanas ate them, but we did not find the taste attractive.

Under the equatorial sun, baked against the black, volcanic earth—which, I sometimes imagined, was turning into molten lava again right under my feet—and with only occasional and extremely thrifty watering, our little *roquette* plants gave us our first mess of home-grown greens within six weeks after they had been sown. They suffered from no diseases and no insects ate them.

I served the first twenty half-grown leaves just as they came from the garden—merely washing them in sea water, which salted them just enough. As we ate our roast goat and rice, each reached for a leaf, then another—watching our turn, so that both of us should get exactly ten leaves—and ate them out of hand, like radishes. The piquant taste of the raw leaves went well with the goat meat—and having grown under tough conditions, our *roquette* was even more peppery than usual. After more of the leaves came on and they grew to full size, I chopped them up into the soup, or cooked them like any other greens—with very little water and giving them only a short cooking time. I felt that we could not afford to waste any of the good qualities of this rare and excellent vegetable.

Though I used leaves from all three kinds of vines I had planted in the "front yard," while those leaves were still young and tender, I could pick fruits from the pumpkin and melon vines only. Beautiful pink moths laid their eggs on the cucumber leaves and blossoms, and the resulting caterpillars killed the plants before we could think of a way to save them. Ainslie sprinkled D.D.T. powder on the melon and pumpkin plants, but we harvested only a dozen pumpkins and eight melons; the rains did not last long enough to keep the plants alive for further production. Our tomato crop was small too—two dozen fruits in all—but they were the best tomatoes we have ever eaten. They would have won no prizes at a show, but they ripened at a time when we were avid for some really heartening fruit. The finches also were fond of them, and I had to pick each fruit as soon as it showed the first signs of ripening.

The gullies were choked with cherry plants during the rainy season, and many came up in Ainslie's little hand-made garden at the spring. There were two varieties of these—one with a white, purple-centred flower, the other blossoming in yellow. The cherries matured soon after the rains had ceased, and I ate handfuls of them, uncooked, every day while they lasted. Ainslie wanted them cooked, so I tried a few pints of jam, which was quite good. Had the birds and insects left these plants alone, we could have canned a thousand pints—if we had had the cans.

We had come to Santiago with four hundred pounds of sugar —surely we did not need to suffer for lack of sweetening. But I did suffer a little as I tried to concoct appetising desserts, especially if I avoided using chocolate. Chocolate and I had clashed before, and it did not take much to revive the old feud.

As a small child I had been very fond of chocolate, perhaps because I tasted it so seldom. Mother did not care for chocolate, and whatever she did not care for, the rest of the family did not get very often. But when I was nearly fourteen, I was sent away from home to attend school—and then chocolate and I really became buddies. On my fifteenth birthday, to celebrate an event no one else seemed to give a hoot about, I went into a bakery and bought a whole, three-layer chocolate cake—the kind that is chocolate all the way through. I ate the entire cake in one afternoon. The next two days I ate nothing at all—and during the following five years mother and I were in almost perfect agreement about chocolate. She could look at it, but I had to turn my eyes away.

As years went by, my taste for the stuff returned, but never again with that first fine fervour. I could like chocolate pretty well if I ate it temperately.

Now, on Santiago, we had a quarter-hundredweight of cocoa and ten pounds of chocolate and few other things to combine with sugar and other ingredients to make a dessert. So chocolate it had to be, a good deal of the time.

Fudge was the easiest concoction—made with chocolate, sugar, a bit of salt, and water. The milk powder we had brought did not last long and was better used for other purposes. It was not necessary to add fat, for none of the oil has been removed from the Ecuadorian variety of chocolate.

Chocolate rice pudding, chocolate galleta pudding, chocolate biscuit pudding, chocolate brownies, chocolate drop cookies, chocolate pancakes, chocolate sauce on rice, chocolate sauce on plain cake, chocolate sauce on chocolate cake, chocolate or cocoa to drink—how often I regretted eating all the way through that chocolate cake on my fifteenth birthday! Ainslie was lucky. He had eaten only vanilla ice cream on his fifteenth birthday, and, on Santiago, neither vanilla, nor ice, nor cream came to taunt him with memories of past indiscretions. There was an exception or two—once we had ice cream: chocolate ice cream. That, of course, had to come as a visitor's gift—it had no other way of arriving.

To get away from chocolate, I flavoured my desserts with spices and whatever else I had the courage to try. Ginger, nutmeg, cinnamon, or cloves were acceptable in the evening drink of sweetened hot water. The same spices served to flavour cakes and puddings—either singly or in combinations. Or I might use ground cherry or water-melon rind preserves as a pudding sauce. I also made pumpkin pudding—as close to the standard filling for pumpkin pie as I could get without milk—candied pumpkin, peanut drop cookies, peanut butter pudding, and peanut brittle.

Not all my desserts were fit for royalty, and many were scarcely fit for the Conways. I cannot decide which was the worst, unless I escape into recklessness and say that after the twentieth chocolate dessert, to me all the chocolate dishes were worst. Yet, my best dessert featured chocolate, too—I made it about the middle of the first month before I had begun remembering my fifteenth birthday too clearly. This unexpected masterpiece was a batch of chocolate pancakes.

I mixed the batter as if I were mixing chocolate cake, but I cannot give the exact measurements, for when you improvise you measure by experience, hunch, guess, and horse-sense. My ingredients were Argentine "lard," sugar, eggs, water, citric acid, baking soda, salt, flour, finely-shaved chocolate, and pinches of cloves and nutmeg. I made the batter thicker than ordinary pancake batter, and baked the cakes slowly in a well-greased aluminium pan, taking great care not to burn them.

These were strictly dessert cakes, and when Ainslie ate them, with many approving words, he stacked them four stories high and flooded them with chocolate sauce. I took mine plain with unsweetened ginger tea.

We never tired of nutmeg nor ginger. I never tired of apricots—that is, of thinking of them and wishing for them. I would also have settled for pineapples, oranges, peaches, or any old fruit. I had dreams of opening a can of apricots, reaching for a spoon to eat them—and never find the spoon. By that time the apricots would have disappeared or I would be awake. Does anyone ever eat anything in his dreams? I never do, though I sometimes dream of food and the intention of eating it.

Once, when I asked Ainslie what he would like to eat if he could have whatever he ordered, he answered without hesitation, "Ham and eggs."

"And what with them?" I persisted.

"A stack of pancakes, I guess."

I was silent while I thought that one over.

IX. SOME RECIPES FOR ENCHANTMENT

SANTIAGO, as I write this, is uninhabited again. Of all the habitable "enchanted" islands, that one is the most "enchanted." Perhaps that is why no one is able, or allowed, to stay on it even semi-permanently. But, during our second venture, while we had it we had it all. "Plenty of real estate," as a visitor remarked—real estate measuring some fifteen by twenty miles, with considerable sea water thrown in. Neither Ecuador, who owns the island, nor the tuna fishermen, who exploit the bait fish in the bays, disturbed our claim and possession in the least.

Yet, jumping-off place though it is, other people at other times had also had it all, or as much of it as they wanted—and that, in most cases, was little enough. In other words, Santiago has a history, which it shares with the other Enchanted Islands.

At that blood-stirring time when gold-laden caravels sailed the Spanish Main, gold-hungry pirates sailed them too, and now and then needed to find a hiding-place to escape pursuit, repair their vessels, or rest from their labours. The Galápagos, where scarcely anyone else cared to go at that epoch, were a perfect haven of refuge. The seas were full of excellent fish—always have been since the Humboldt Current started flowing, and always will be, we presume, as long as California tuna fishermen hope and pray—the land was simply crawling with sweet-fleshed galápagos and iguanas, and sufficient water was to be had too if you were lucky enough to find it. There is evidence that the pirates stocked some of the islands with goats and cattle and planted fruit trees. Why not? Even a pirate cannot eat pieces of eight and gold necklaces. There are stories too that pirates buried treasure in the Galápagos and documents show that they cached flour and quince jam among the rocks of a certain shore on one occasion. It could have been at James Bay.

Later British and Yankee whalers discovered the virtues of the Humboldt Current and the virtues of galápago meat and oil—and what adventures in those days! First a voyage around the Horn—an enchanted voyage, as the Ancient Mariner had learned, and then a landfall in the Encantadas!

No wonder Captain David Porter, of the U.S. Navy,

not resist "exceeding his orders" and rounding the Horn himself in 1813, to make single-handed war on the British whaling fleet. No doubt Porter believed that he was engaged in patriotic and dutiful work, but I am convinced that patriotism and sense of duty did not guide him to the Galápagos. Enchantment called him, though a naval man could not admit it.

Porter left an American grave near the shore at James Bay. In that "corner of a foreign field" lies Lieutenant Cowan, U.S.N., who was silly enough to lose his life in a duel. When President Roosevelt came cruising to the Galápagos in 1938, he sent a party ashore to look for the grave, but the searchers found nothing.

Incidentally, during his stay at James Bay, Porter did a good turn for us, though it started as a bad turn for himself. He put his milch goats ashore to graze, and they wandered away and were not found again. Those historical goats were the ancestors of the animals we were eating in such great numbers.

When officers of the British Navy came to chart the islands in 1835, Charles Darwin came along to have a look at the animals. On James Island he found thousands of land iguanas, of which we found not one, and a group of Spanish-speaking galápago hunters encamped on the shore and in the mountains. Some years later a salt-gathering expedition made a serious effort to exploit the deposits in the crater lake, but this venture met the fate of most other Galápagos money-making attempts. In our time the salt-gatherers' abandoned machinery still rusted on the edge of the crater and their roads made easy travelling on the James Bay flatlands.

The next known attempt to colonise Santiago had been our own. That first time we had not come alone, but—through no choice of ours—accompanied by three other family groups: an unattached Hungarian named Grafi, a young German and his Ecuadorian wife, whom we had known as Alfredo and América, and a Chilean with a wife and eight children. The Chilean was named and titled Captain-Engineer Humberto Goya Rico, and he had lived long enough in Ecuador to commit some sort of political misdemeanour. The Ecuadorian officials, at their wits' end what to do with him and his retinue, had hit upon the expedient of sending them to exile in the Galápagos.

Grafi, a foot-loose adventurer, had come to Santiago with sufficient provisions and equipment to live in comparative comfort for the duration of his stay. The German had furniture and a few tools, but he had run out of money before he could provide himself with food. Goya Rico, who was rich in family only, had nothing else of value—no tools, no building materials, no clothing except what the family carried on their backs, and no food. As a prisoner he expected the Ecuadorian government to provide for him—though he should have known better. At that time we did not have much either, but we had sufficient rice, sugar, flour, beans, and coffee to last us six or eight months, and the most necessary and useful tools—machete, axe, saw, hammer, pliers, hunting knives, pick, shovel, rake—and a few odds and ends, like rope, wire, and nails.

Grafi was the only person who possessed a usable gun. The German had two dogs and—for no sensible reason—a couple of ocelots in cages. All except the Goya Rico family had several chickens, the German had two turkeys, and the Conways had two ducks and two donkeys. On San Cristóbal we had purchased banana, pineapple, yuca, sugar-cane, and *camote* plants and cuttings to start *chacras* for all groups. Grafi had also brought a small boat, and all of us had some sort of fishing tackle and garden seeds.

Fortunately for the captain-engineer and his family, an old house of bamboo and tar paper still remained at James Bay, built there many years ago by salt gatherers. Considering the pleasant climate, the house was good enough—probably larger and better than any house the family had previously occupied. The beach where it stood we now call the Goya Rico Beach, and the spring which furnished the family with water, though they had to carry it nearly two miles, is known as the Goya Rico spring.

The other three families established themselves about a mile inland from the Goya Rico Beach, near a small spring which happened to be producing water at that time. In this area, which is part of what I like to call the Pleasant Belt, Grafi, the German, and we built rain-shelters as best we could—only Grafi had roofing iron to cover his *chala*-pole house-frame, and Alfredo and Ainslie roofed theirs with bur-grass thatch. Each group started a garden—Goya Rico on his beach, and the rest of us around our so-called houses. It was then the beginning of the eight-months dry season on the lower land-levels of the Galápagos, and we could not expect much food from these gardens for many months.

We led a partially communal existence—the German and Grafi hunted and fished, Goya Rico and his family did the butchering and meat delivering, and the Conways received their meat the easy way for the first two months—simply in exchange for the seeds and plant-cuttings we had allotted equally to every-body. Each group, however, cleared, planted, and cared for their own garden and, except for a little tool-borrowing, designed and built—or repaired—their own house.

Within two months, Grafi and the German and América had gone back to Guayaquil on an Ecuadorian fishing boat which happened to choose James Bay for her operations. Grafi was ready to go, because he had come merely to get acquainted with the island, and the German and his wife were more than ready, for they had soon tired of living on goat meat, pork, and fish and nothing else—not even coffee, which might have made life on Santiago, especially to the coffee-loving Alfredo, almost worth living. Upon leaving, Grafi and Alfredo had sold the most useful of their equipment to us—Alfredo had taken his furniture and the ocelots with him.

Goya Rico and the Conways remained—the captain-engineer because, as a prisoner, he had to stay even though goat and fish were becoming a bit appalling to him too—and the Conways because they had come to the island to live there as long as circumstances or the Ecuadorian government allowed. Conway now had his turn hunting—catching goats alive with the help of the dogs—Goya Rico continued butchering, and life on the island went on very much as it had started.

However, after three months, the Ecuadorian government remembered the exiled family of Goya Rico, whom it had promised to keep in reasonable victuals, and sent the old gun-boat *Calderón* to see how the desert island babies were getting along. The territorial governor, who had his headquarters on San Cristóbal, came with the ship. He was a headstrong, tem-peramental *caballero*, who liked to do things his own way and then wash his hands. Instead of letting Goya Rico serve the rest of his sentence on Santiago, where he wanted to stay as long as we were there, the governor found it expedient to move him to another island, where, presumably, the family could scrape up a better-balanced diet—the *Calderón*, as usual, had no food to spare. This time too, in order to quiet the captain-engineer's erudite and voluble objections and protests, he let the latter choose whichever other island he preferred. The captain-engineer preferred no other. The governor, in his impulsive way, suddenly decided to evacuate the Conways, too, saying that he did not feel it harmonious with his moral obligation as territorial governor to leave them alone on a "dangerous" island, and gave them their choice of another island. After trying a few protests on our part, we agreed to go to Floreana. Goya Rico, to whom we seemed to be mascots as well as friends, decided to go with us.

With the memory of this first, unexpectedly curtailed sojourn on Santiago to guide us, we planned several excursions to spots we had previously known and approved, and a longer trip to the mountains, where I had never been before. Ainslie dreamed of an extended exploring expedition into the high country, but he did not consider it wise to go alone or to leave me unaccompanied on the beach for many days, and he kept hoping that some adventurous-minded visitors might one day appear and be willing to go on that expedition with him

During the first weeks of our second stay on Santiago, Ainslie covered a good deal of territory in the course of his hunting treks for water and goat. One day, when he had energy to spare, he climbed Sugar Loaf, thinking it possible that the crater contained water. All Ainslie saw from the high, rocky, windy rim were the sandstone sides of the crater-cup, covered sparsely with *palos santos* and shrubs and sloping down rather steeply, and a level, grassy bottom where a dozen goats were grazing. Though a little moisture may have been present down below, the prospect was not promising enough to warrant the hazards and troubles of investigating. Ainslie's greatest reward for the climb was a view of a large part of Santiago and so much blue ocean that he became conscious of the parching thirst his efforts had given him.

The first tour of exploration I made with Ainslie—if I don't count fishing trips to the coastal rocks—was a sort of ceremonial visit we made one Sunday to Coral Bay. We had seen Coral Bay once before—and named it—ten years ago, and, ever since, had longed to go back. As we might have known, we did not find it quite as we had left it; even in the Galápagos change is one of the certainties of life.

What we remembered was a flow of lava, not too new, between Sugar Loaf and Little Sugar Loaf—the latter is a somewhat smaller crater almost identical in shape and formation with the larger Sugar Loaf—a view of green mountains beyond the source of the lava, and in the opposite direction a beach of white coral, blue tidal pools framed with black lava, white surf—and then the ocean, blue and sparkling, and, as if floating on it in the distance, the hazy, violet craters of Isabela. The breeze had been fresh and the sun brilliant over everything.

All this we found, more or less, but without most of the

glamour and brilliance.   The glamour was dimmed because we
had expected too much and because the novelty was gone.   After
all, we had seen this place before—it was now like the second
piece of cake, not the first.   The day was dull, warm, and
cloudy, and, unfortunately, the tide was out, leaving the pools
waterless.   Mangrove had grown all over the white coral beach
and pushed its salt-water sucking roots into the pools.   It
seemed, too, that there was more black lava than I remembered
—or could it be that I was growing very, very unfond of black
lava?

We lingered a couple of hours, however, for Ainslie was
intrigued by the fiddler crabs among the mangrove roots and
the tide-pool fishlets left to gasp in the lava basins.   I searched
for additions to my oddment collection and found several beautiful pieces of coral, shells not seen on the James Bay beaches,
and a couple of usable tin cans.   We both looked for our
friends, the sea iguanas, of which we had seen at least three
dozen on our first visit.   Only a few pelicans and a moody-
looking blue heron dozed on the rocks.   They had probably
eaten so many fishlets and crabs that they could not stay awake,
much less fly.

On the way home we came upon a good cord of *aromo* wood,
cut into four-foot lengths, and neatly stacked.   Something else
to wonder about.   Who had cut this wood, when, and for what
purpose?   And why so far from the beach, when there was
plenty of other *aromo* wood much nearer?   We could have used
it, but it was too far from El Corral to be worth the trouble of
transportation.

Our second long walk together was also *in memoriam*.   This
time we followed a straggling donkey trail, skirting Sugar Loaf
eastward, in the direction of the spring that had furnished us
with water in 1937.   Grafi and the German had lived right by
this water-hole, and we had had our grass-thatched rain-shelter,
our outdoor kitchen, and our garden clearing some thirty rods
away in the, then, fairly thick jungle of shrubbery, trees, and lianas.

Approaching the spring, we entered the Pleasant Belt—and
found it still pleasant, though much of the shrubbery that Ainslie
and Alfredo had once fought with machetes was dead and dry
now and lying on the ground.   The trees were still standing,
however, thick with new green leaves, and the sunlight was
bright.   We had chosen a good day for this visit, a March day
when the rainy season was two months old.

The little water-hole which has so much meaning for us, and no meaning whatever for almost anyone else, is at the bottom of a shallow sandstone gully and white-barked, spiritual-looking *palos santos* grow around it. Here, ten years ago, Ainslie had picked out a rectangular hole in the rock to catch the seepage—a hole large enough to hold twenty gallons. We found it now filled with rocks and sand. Ainslie began to clear the rubble out and saw that the rocks had been piled in neatly, as if by a human hand. No doubt some Ecuadorian fishermen or *gringo* yachtsmen had done this to keep the animals from drinking up all the water that collected. The sand at the bottom of the hole was moist, showing that a very thin trickle of water was still seeping in.

While Ainslie was cleaning the water-hole I went visiting—at Grafi's and Alfredo's. Or was it América I wanted to see?

Grafi's house had stood on a little knoll above the spring. Nothing was left to indicate that any sort of habitation had ever been there. But I knew I was in the right place—I found the two large slabs of lava that Grafi had used for a fireplace.

Alfredo's place evoked more memories. He had made a good garden clearing and planted it with bananas, papayas, sugar-cane, corn, yuca, and potatoes. América had planted the seeds of a few trees she had brought from Guayaquil. The clearing was still clear, but weeds and grass had taken the place of the imported vegetation. I recognised the thorn bushes on which América had been in the habit of hanging her washing—she had washed every day. I imagined that I could smell the very odours that used to cling to the air around América's grass-roofed bed-room—odours of dead fish and live goat. Though perhaps the odour of goat was not imaginary, after all. The clearing was plaided with their trails, and the trails were written over with their hoof-tracks.

As I picked the red-black berries with which the thorn bushes were covered and crammed them into my mouth, I felt a curious nostalgia, not for Alfredo and América but for the time when we had known them. It seemed that ten years ago had been somewhere far back in our early youth, and this abandoned *chacra*-site was exceedingly lonely—not because no one was living in it, but because someone had lived there once and never would return.

"If you are going to start mooning over what once was and now is not," I told myself, "please save your sentiment for that other place a bit farther on. Perhaps there you will find something more substantial for sentiment to feed on." After picking a final handful of the berries, I went back to the spring where Ainslie was trying to measure the scarcely perceptible trickle into the catchment basin.

Ainslie put the rocks back into the basin—the reason for this precaution was not quite clear—and with mixed reluctance and eagerness we took the donkey-trail eastward, toward the spot where we had built our first Santiago home. It had been, in fact, our first joint home anywhere.

Upon entering the clearing which had once cost Ainslie so much machete work, I glanced at his face to read his mood and thoughts. He was poker-faced and silent, which with him often means that he is bursting with emotion. What emotion at this moment? The same futile nostalgia which I felt, not for a place —for here we were—but for a time gone by, an episode and an experience that could not be lived again?

In the bright noon sunshine the place was lovely even in its abandoned state. The leafy, yellow-blossomed *muyuyus*, the fragrant *palos santos*, and much of the enclosing shrubbery were as we had left them. The earth, which we had last seen cleared of all wild growth and planted with bananas, yuca, *camotes*, and pineapples, was now entirely covered with trailing plants which spread over it like a green carpet strewn with small purple flowers.

As we walked toward the centre of this little green-bright meadow, where our "house *muyuyu*" and grass-thatched house had been, some words from a poem by Marti kept running through my head—"*Tierra del sol amada, tierra del sol amada, tierra del sol amada*"—only those words, like an incantation. "Land of the sun beloved"—owned and loved by the sun, but no longer owned—merely loved—by us. Why so beloved by us? We could not have felt so homesick for a palace, had we once had it and lost it. Why yearn for this piece of desert then? Neither of us wept, but either of us could have, if we had been there alone. In eath other's presence, we had to keep our dignity.

The house *muyuyu* was leaning even farther toward the earth than it had been when we lived under its shade—for only three short, short months, after all—but it was vigorous and blooming still. On its trunk and limbs I found the nails I had used for pot and clothes hooks, and on one of these was a clothes-hanger with my name on it—the only usable thing we had forgotten to take with us before we embarked for Floreana. On the ground I saw two large shells and some pieces of coral I had collected at Coral Bay when we visited it the first time. I did not stoop to pick them up.

A little to one side was my lava rock fireplace. How naïve and childish it looked! And more sentiment-stirring than anything else was a pathetic pile of firewood, sticks I had gathered in the jungle, broken over my knee, and piled up neatly. The wood was quite as I had left it, not decayed, nor disturbed in any way. "Enchanted sticks," I said inwardly, and then added: "What a silly thought!"

"For heaven's sake, look at the firewood!" I said to Ainslie, who was saying not a word, and pointed to those touching leftovers, as if laughing at the play-house furniture of a child. But I was not laughing, nor was Ainslie. I was mourning over the child who had "put them there," and the child was myself.

The house had fallen down, and the grass thatch had long since become loam, but the *chala* poles Ainslie had chopped out of the jungle, carried home—home, indeed!—on his shoulder, and wired together, were still intact, though lying on the ground. I was about to pick up some of the wire as a souvenir, then thought: "What need have we of souvenirs? Just leave the wire here, and whatever else you find. Looting the dead is desecration."

"How would you like to come back and spend the night here under that *muyuyu* where we made our bed when we camped in this place the first time?" I asked Ainslie. I had been asking myself the same question, but could not answer yes or no.

Ainslie shook his head. "The beds at El Corral are much more comfortable," his tongue said, pretending to be practical. But the look in his eyes cried out: "I could not sleep here. Our own ghosts would haunt us. The ghosts of dead donkeys, of dead goats, of dead doves, of dead mocking-birds, of dead lizards, of dead finches—perhaps even the ghosts of dead bushes —would come to haunt us. A dead moon would shine, and a thousand thousand dead stars——! God, I cannot take any more of this!" Then his tongue said: "Let's walk down to the Goya Rico Beach."

And so we left our first desert island home—enchanted home on an enchanted island—as we had found it, and as we had left it—was it ten thousand years ago? So far away it was, and so long ago, that we could never find our way back to it again.

If anyone should care to ask why we made such a big event of revisiting an abandoned home site, scarcely more than a camp site—a couple of weed-grown acres too far from water to be

H

liveable, we would simple retort: Have you ever built a house of grass and sticks on an uninhabited island—a desert island ten thousand miles from your former home grounds and from everything else you had previously seen or experienced? And was that spot of desert the first home you ever owned? And have you ever been suddenly torn away from such a place, much against your will? And have you ever waited ten years and travelled ten thousand miles to see that bit of earth again?

Gradually our mood cleared as we approached Playa Goya Rico—memories of the captain-engineer and his brood were always mercifully lightened with humour. Ainslie's old trail was gone—or rather, so much widened by droughts that we could not recognise it as a trail—and we had an open road in almost any direction. Near the beach heavy washes had made a deep channel through Goya Rico's garden and carried away most of the good soil.

Nothing was left of the Villa Goya Rico—Don Humberto had insisted on taking most of the house with him when he was moved to Floreana, and Ecuadorian fishermen had spirited away the rest. We had selfishly exhausted our emotions over our own relics, and now were merely curious. No thought of desecration entered our minds here, and for my oddment collection I picked up a battered wash-pan and a shrivelled leather shoe that had belonged to Oslavia, the oldest Goya Rico *señorita*. It was flimsy and high-heeled and had once been bright blue— meant for afternoon strolls on the streets of Guayaquil.

As we searched along the beach for any other memory-evoking rubbish, we saw a tuna ship headed toward the harbour. Promptly we took off along the sandstone pavement for home, thinking that the fishermen might anchor and come ashore. But by the time we reached our own beach, the ship had turned around and was pulling out seaward again.

That was the day the grey hen had laid an egg on Ainslie's bed. We took it as a consolation.

X. TO THE JUST AND THE UNJUST MOUNTAINS

Iт was the middle of March before we finally found the courage to cross the lava flow in the direction of the high mountains. The previous day and many days before it had been exceptionally hot, and we had stayed in one spot too long, worked at routine chores too steadily, looked on the same scene too often, and spent too much emotion on souvenirs of past adventure. The cure for our condition was a change of scene and climate.

As we drank our coffee that morning, a little after six o'clock when the sun was just peering over the mountains, Ainslie was silent and I was silent. I suppose both of us knew that if we spoke we would end by quarrelling; either one or the other would say something to arouse the other's latent irritability. On our beach it was already hot—in fact, we had slept that night with only a sweat-damp sheet to cover us. I looked toward the mountains, still mist-shrouded, and thought: "Looks cool enough. I wonder why we can't go up there."

"After all," I said to Ainslie, my voice none too pleasant, "we have been on this island for months and we have not been in the mountains yet. We aren't under contract to fritter and fry on this beach until we are a couple of burnt offerings." I wanted to blame somebody for my feeling of discomfort and ennui.

Ainslie understood that he was that somebody. "Okay," he said with a sort of desperate, threatening patience. "We are going right this minute."

I had not thought of going quite that soon, but since the glove had been thrown down I had to pick it up. I felt desperate too. "Suits me," I said. "We'd better take a canteen of water."

And so we were off, after putting the premises in order and blocking the front gate with the table and a couple of large rocks. We wore our usual scanty clothes—shorts, sun-glasses, hats, and, out of respect for the long journey, shirts. I forgot, in my stirred-up state, to change my old leather shoes for rubber-soled sneakers. On lava, a good Galápagan walks on rubber or on incredibly calloused, live sole leather. At his belt Ainslie carried a quart jar of water in a little khaki bag, and in his right hand a machete.

Our trail took us first in the direction of the Salt Lake Crater. The walk from Goya Rico Beach to this crater is the most charming in all the Galápagos, for it leads through the Pleasant Belt. The charm is considerably marred during two or three months following the rainy season, for then the bur-grass is in the seed-bearing stage. These seeds are prickly and marvellously adapted to being carried about on the hair, clothes, and skin of the passer-by. However, in March, though the grass was tall and green, it had not yet gone to seed. The *palos santos* were now as green as apple trees in June and as aromatic as they can be. This region is one of the very few in the Encantadas where a man can walk upright and free, as he should, and worry little about thorn-entanglements and boulders.

Before we had gone a mile our road was in fragrant shade. And road is what I mean, for the salt gatherers had built a good passage—one may even call it a highway—and no brush had grown up in recent years to mar it. A fresh breeze had come up before eight o'clock, tree finches and mocking-birds were singing, and we forgot all about our early morning irritation.

On all sides we startled fat goats, and donkeys, for these wise beasts had returned to the lower altitudes as soon as the rains had started. They ran a little on seeing us and the dog, and then turned around to huff and snort. The goats were mostly black or red, with white markings. Some, otherwise coal black, had brilliant white hind quarters. The donkeys were large, smooth-coated, either light grey or dark brown with black manes and shoulder stripes. One very dark stallion wore a wide band of white around his muzzle and around each eye. He looked like a clown, though he gave us a gallant "How do you do?" when he saw us. We hee-hawed back at him.

Trees grew thicker and larger as we approached the crater —a gain in altitude always means a gain in moisture in the Galápagos. There were large, leafy *muyuyus* and *palos santos,* but fewer *aromos* as we advanced. *Aromos* are evidently drought-loving trees. We also passed a couple of *algarobos,* which are not common on Santiago. These specimens may have sprouted from seeds carried here from other islands—in the pockets of people or in the intestines of animals. One large tree I had never seen before—it was large and stout-looking, with smooth, reddish-grey bark, and rounded, short-stemmed leaves. But most interesting to me was a little, battered-up fruit tree—I had never seen one like it before either. The tree was older than the size indicated; several older stems had died, and the present stem was only a "sucker." The animals had probably been nibbling at it ever since it sprouted, whenever that may have been.

This fruit tree was definitely not native to the island, or to any of the other islands, and must have grown from a seed casually thrown down or intentionally planted. The fruit was

like a small plum, greenish-yellow in colour and very acid, though not unpleasant in taste. At first I was afraid to pick any of the fruit, thinking the tree might be a *manzanillo*, which is native to the islands. The sap of the *manzanillo* is corrosive, and many Galápagan Ecuadorians carry its scars on their skins. (We had met one who had a white, ugly, totally blind eye as a result of receiving a squirt of *manzanillo* sap into it.) Ainslie told me that this "plum" tree was quite harmless, but I did not trust his knowledge. However, when I noticed that the animals had picked up all the fallen fruit and trampled the grass under the tree, I believed that this was no *manzanillo*. Each of us picked some of the fruit—we just had to eat some of this rare Santiago product—and agreed to pick more on our way home.

A little farther on were a few *muyuyu de arriba*, which are different from the yellow-blossomed *muyuyus*. This variety is not exactly a vine, but it likes to lean on sturdier trees and bears coarse, dark-green leaves—which Ainslie had often smoked in place of tobacco when we lived on Floreana—and clusters of white flowers. Several shrubs and trees were unknown to us —among them a curious, small tree with a red berry in a pod that opened out in three sections. I tasted the berry and found it sweet and insipid.

A sharp rise in the trail took us to the edge of the crater, and we looked down. *Palos santos* and shrubbery lined the bowl to the rim, but at the bottom, around the little pool, was a brilliant green circle of grass, *monte salado,* and *manzanillo*. The shallow water reflected the blue sky, but beneath we could see a sort of cracked pavement of pink, green, grey, and white. The white represented salt, though we could not account for the pastel tints. The greener-than-green *manzanillo* leaves shone like satin in the sunlight, and the *monte salado* had been "pruned" by goats until the bushes looked like hand-shaped creations of Italian gardeners. We had expected to see pink flamingos, but there were none. Only a black hawk flew over the crater screaming.

The region around the crater had that exotic Santiago atmosphere, but intensified—an aura which combined elements of classic mythology and of the mesozoic era, with something of primeval chaos thrown in. Far away we seemed to be, infinitely far away and long ago.

Pan could have peeped out from among the bushes at any time—perhaps he did peep out. Pan was half-goat, and as we stared into the green-rimmed eye of the salt pool, three bucks —black, long-horned, bearded—slipped out of the *manzanillo* thickets and approached the classically-pruned masses of *monte salado*. They stood on their hind legs, straight up like half-human creatures, and snatched good salty mouthfuls of the coarse leaves. A wild ass brayed and was answered by another so far away that his raucous call came to us as music.

At our feet grew strange grasses, a centipede combed his way through it and hid under a strange bush. A red-throated lizard came to sun herself on Ainslie's shoe, and we thought of the galápagos and iguanas that had only recently crawled around this crater—relics of an age millions of years past.

From the corner of my eye—now that I was so close to it, I did not want to look on it—I could see the lava flow. I felt a vague horror of that tortured sheet of burned-out rock—it seemed so broad now, so very black, grotesque and horrible. Beyond lay the ocean, blue, flat, empty, utterly unconcerned, utterly lost in its own existence. It had not changed since the day it was created.

All this was not of now—it was something that had once been, and by enchantment its mirage had been left here for us

to gaze at, an illusion only, a trick of the cosmic ether—a mirage that sneered at time as ordinary mirages sneer at space.

"Look over there," I said to Ainslie, pointing at the northern horizon. "What island is that?"

"It can't be Pinta, but it must be Pinta," he answered, as if a little startled.

"But how far is Pinta? I thought I saw an island there the other day, but knowing there was no island there, I told myself that it was a cloud."

"It's Pinta all right, though that island is at least sixty miles from here, and now it seems to lie only a couple of miles beyond Albany."

"So, a mirage. I was just thinking of mirages. No wonder the early navigators thought these islands rose and sank."

"I suppose, if they saw one like that—sixty miles away but appearing to be as close as eight miles—and the next time did not see it at all, they concluded that the island was bewitched. Add to that poor navigation, and the result is the enchanted islands."

"Have you perchance seen the enchanted isles rise from the sea where uncounted miles of water lie as when land was not—— Now what do I say?"

"When the wind was cool and the sun was hot, and we stared in the face of the lava flow—but *tempus fugit*, and we have to go."

"The rhyme is not too bad, but the lava flow—what is the landmark you are aiming at on the other side?" I was already wishing I were on the other side.

"The cinder cone near the lower edge of that tree-grown old crater on the nearest mountain-side."

"That means we cross diagonally—and so stay on the lava longer."

"Yes, but we'll probably save time. I've dreamed for ten years of revisiting that crater. It was Alfredo's paradise, remember—all overgrown with great, strange, leafy trees, and a pig under every tree."

I too had dreamed of seeing that crater—I had not seen it as Ainslie had—because at one time we had planned to make a plantation there. We had thought it would be about the most exotic home-site in the world. "But it looks rather queer now," I said. "It is not nearly so green any more—it has a curious, grey, tangled look. What do you think is the matter up there?"

"Don't know, but we'll find out. Ready to go?"

I rose reluctantly, but I could not hesitate. After all, I had insisted on this trip. Ainslie too seemed reluctant, though he did not say so. He now studied the surface of the flow and indicated the way it would be best to go—keep away from the very blackest part, where he said the lava was finely cut up like shattered glass (I remembered the worn leather soles of my shoes now) and follow the areas where the surface was a little greyer and formed into waves, like the swell on open sea.

With grim determination, but also with that exhilaration that attends all adventure, we gathered up the machete, called the dog, and marched down the side of the crater—through very thick brush now—and before I was quite ready for it, stopped at the edge of the lava.   Then we scrambled up on it—I had to use my hands to help my feet, for the lava lay rather thick even on the edges—five or six feet at this spot.

At the centre the flow was much thicker—it had devastated a fair valley.   I asked Ainslie how deep he thought it might be in the deepest places, but he too could only guess.   Roughly we estimated the depth might reach fifty feet—perhaps much more if the valley had been deeper than it now appeared to have been.

From the edge to the farther side now seemed a longer distance than I cared to estimate.   Perhaps two miles along our projected route, but the actual walking distance would be much more—even a donkey could see that there would be much twisting and turning and going up and down.   We had a watch with us and noted the time.   When we had reached the other side—I hoped we would eventually get there, though I was not sure—we could better judge the distance from the time it took us to cross.

At first I was fairly confident.   The lava lay in smooth waves and the cracks were not wider than my stride could easily span. I made note of the colour of the fissures—the black was only on the surface and farther down it shaded into grey, rust, and maroon.   I had not the heart to peer very far down, and anyhow a few feet from the top it was too dark to see anything.   Ainslie led the way, for he had more experience and a surer foot.   He wore sneakers with thick rubber soles, and I was increasingly conscious that I walked on thin, worn leather.   Lava cuts leather very easily.

After travelling only a few rods I realised that the crossing would be tiring, not because each step required so much energy —after all, we were not wading in deep mud or fighting our way through tangled undergrowth—but because we had to be alert and watchful every moment.   I dared not raise my eyes to look around unless I came to a full stop first.   A false step was so easy and it might be disastrous.   I imagined Ainslie with a broken leg out in the middle of the lava—how far that middle still seemed!—and immediately clicked the picture out.   Better wait to imagine things like that until after the crossing had been made, or—better still—until the return crossing had been completed.   I preferred not to think of the return crossing. "Tomorrow," I told myself, "you will be glad you did this—something, surely, that no other *señora* has ever done—so keep on stepping, and watch your step."

I concentrated on stepping—no trouble concentrating, for I

could not help it.   As we neared the centre area the waves
became higher and rougher.   I stopped to look around.   I
seemed to be in the centre of a choppy Gulf of Tehuantepec—
that gulf is a chronically rough spot on the Pacific coast of
Mexico—a Tehuantepec suddenly frozen and turned black in
the middle of a storm.   Exactly that.   Imagine a black, con-
gealed, choppy sea and you have it—also you have another
illusion of enchantment.   All you need to add are wide and
who knows how deep fissures and now and again a buckled spot
—where huge blocks of ragged rock had been pushed up and
out of line by uneven cooling and shrinkage.   One of our
troubles was avoiding the buckled spots and finding a way
around them.   Several times I travelled on all fours, not trusting
myself upright on the edges of fissures or while climbing over
steep, broken-up hillocks.

In the centre of the flow there were so many crevices and
buckles that we were forced out of our planned line of march
and on to one of those places we had meant to avoid—the
"crushed glass" areas.   There were no high breakers and wide
cracks and jumbled buckles here, but something perhaps worse
unless you were wearing extremely heavy shoes.   The lava was
so crushed and brittle that it crackled under foot—"cinders of
glass" might describe it.   I could feel the hard, cutting edges
through my shoes and I walked on this devil's pavement as
delicately as I could.   Fortunately, we did not need to stay on
it long—a good stretch of solid, though none too smooth, lava
appeared ahead.

Now that we were half-way over, and, as I thought, the worst
had been safely passed, I began to observe things that had at
first escaped me.   The sky had clouded over us, though I could
see that in the vicinity of Sugar Loaf and El Corral it was still
clear.   This was a mercy; crossing the lava under the March sun
might have been more purgatory than we cared to foretaste.

We found donkey and goat droppings, but only in the
smoother places—evidently the animals knew where the best
going was.   In a crevice was the skeleton of a kid who had
not been as nimble as he thought, or perhaps he had been
crowded or pushed.   Odd foxtail-like cactus grew in the most
seemingly impossible spots—in sheer, stony lava—and some
cracks harboured coarse, stringy grass; at any rate, it looked
like grass.

And there were odd formations in the lava itself.   In some
places the rock was twisted into long ropes, and now and again

the ropes were braided.   These were interesting, but there were also troughs and bubbles, which were even more interesting because to me they were terrible.   The troughs were places where the molten stream of lava had formed a thin crust as it cooled on top but had kept on flowing underneath until only the crust was left.   The bubbles were about the same except that they were not so elongated in shape but often were much deeper. Though I tried hard to avoid it, I sometimes stepped on the thin crust of a bubble and it broke sickeningly under foot.   None of the bubbles I stepped on were very deep—not more than a foot —but they kept me worried.   How was I to know that the next one would not be ten feet deep—and then where would I be?

The last half of the crossing took us upward—we were climbing the lava-covered lower slope of the mountain range. We could tell the difference in the air already—it must have been a good fifteen degrees cooler than it was at that moment in El Corral.   Wisps of mist blew over us and the mountains ahead were cloud-covered.

"We'll get wet," Ainslie said.   Ainslie always hates to be caught in a rain.

"Yes, we'll get wet," I repeated, but not in the same tone of voice.   Sometimes I like to get caught in a rain.

At this higher altitude there was more vegetation, even on the lava.   In some wider cracks grew grass, ferns, and ground cherries.   A few stubborn shrubs, resembling heather, had managed a foothold, possibly in places where the lava was thin. All at once we came to a place where a tree-top seemed to be pushing up through the black rock.   Ainslie went boldly ahead to investigate—I followed slowly and cautiously, feeling my way. That tree, I thought, must be growing in a hole, and I was not in the mood to trust holes.

I did not go as near the hole as Ainslie did, though I went near enough to see that it was roundish, some twelve feet in diameter and about the same depth or a little more.   The tree —one of the pinky-grey barked species we had seen near the salt crater and which we could not name—was about twenty feet tall and grew right in the middle of the space at the bottom, which, no doubt, was earth.   Ferns, moss, nettles, and ground cherries crowded around the roots of the tree and hung down from every little crevice at the sides of the hole.   A lovely little rock-walled garden, but it gave me the shivers, because I could not help but imagine myself down in that garden too.   I started to back away—and remembered just in time. Garden or no garden, I was still on the lava—and I must look before I step. I turned around conscientiously and walked away watching my feet.

We were now nearing the upper edge of the flow and skirting the cinder cone which was our landmark. The cone was higher than I had estimated at a distance—some thirty feet high perhaps —and black as a pile of anthracite. We could smell the *palos santos* and hear the finches singing in the trees ahead. Only a few rods now, but they proved to be bad rods. This last stretch was one bubble after another, and I nearly had the horrors. I thought I smelled sulphur as the bubbles cracked under my feet. When the lava ended we looked at the watch. The crossing had taken us an hour and ten minutes.

Off the open lava flow and into a thick forest of large trees was one step. This was melodrama. The slope slanted well upward, and as we climbed, pushing aside wet branches, we were soon climbing over the trunks of great fallen trees. The higher we went, toward the entrance of the tree-filled old crater, the thicker were the prostrate giants. These were all of the species we must call Nameless Trees—with beautiful rosy-grey bark and roundish leaves. Plenty of forest was still upright, however —younger Nameless specimens, *palos santos*, or their very close relatives, and slender, straight strangers with nearly white bark —they reminded me of birches. Their straightness fascinated us. In all our years in the Galápagos we had never seen so many straight trees at one glance.

We came to the entrance of the cuplike valley that was the bottom of the old crater we had come to see—and here were more and still more fallen trees—all Nameless. Only a few younger ones remained upright. This, then, was the explanation for that curious, grey, tangled look which had puzzled us.

"You can imagine what this was like when all these trees were standing, as they were ten years ago," Ainslie said. "I never saw a place like it. There was no underbrush—only these great trees. Except for the finches singing everything was perfectly quiet."

I could imagine. This must have been a fairy forest. I could agree with friend Alfredo, who had gone daffy about the place when he first saw it and said to me: "It is just like Paradise!" But now a bomb seemed to have fallen on paradise.

"What do you suppose happened here?" I asked Ainslie. "If the flyers from the base used this crater for target practice, the bombs would have wrecked all the trees and left holes in the earth—or would they?"

"Can't have been a bomb.   Not even drought.   That would have killed the smaller trees too, and all over the mountains, not only here."

"Volcanic action?" I suggested.   "That cinder cone is pretty close.   And, yet, sulphur fumes—or whatever fumes volcanoes are in the habit of belching out—would also have killed other trees."

"The only reasonable cause I can think of is exceptionally heavy rain.   The earth could have been so softened by downpours that the old roots could no longer hold the overweight crowns upright.   Or perhaps old age had something to do with it."

"I hate to see them down like this," Ainslie said after we had stepped over more dozens of prostrate trunks, "but if we were to make a plantation here, the land would now be much easier to clear.   Less axework necessary."

"I doubt that you would have had the heart to cut down these trees, anyway—or if you had, you would have mourned over them."

"Yes, though I would have had consolation.   With the trees cleared out, the view from here is marvellous."

I turned to look westward—the only direction for a view, for the sides of the crater and the mountain behind it shut out every other vista.   Only a few trees stood in the way now, and I could see ahead of me the Pleasant Belt, the two Sugar Loaves, the bay, the ocean, and Isabela—but before my eyes could take delight in those things they had to cross the frozen, black sea of lava, which lay practically on the doorstep.   And the lava would have to be crossed or skirted each time we moved out of the plantation.   Perhaps in time I could become used to it.   Also perhaps not.   Yet I could not quite say no to this place.   Where on earth could there be another home-site like this one, and who on earth would want it—except us, probably—an overlush crater bottom at the edge of a raw lava flow perhaps less than fifty years old?   (No one seems to know the exact age of the James Bay flow, though some say it was born in 1907.)

However, this was not the moment to make a decision.   We pushed the thought of plantation making into the bottom drawer, and turned to skirt the slope northward.   Going was a scramble at first—there were few boulders but still plenty of fallen trunks and that thick, tangled growth which is typical of the edges of

forests.   Presently it began to rain, quietly but steadily.   The air
was thick with a spicy fragrance, and a million finches kept on
singing.

Ainslie, as usual, had his eye out for a trail, and we found
one very soon—a goat and donkey trail that led off along the
edge of the lava toward the east arm of James Bay.   This arm
ends in a fair-sized mountain we were in the habit of calling "Old
Crater"—which describes it exactly, as it would describe any
mountain in the Galápagos.   We had heard reports that there
was a spring on the landward side of the crater, and, in our
opinion, this trail eventually wound up at that water-hole.   The
distance to the hypothetical spring, from where we were, was
several miles along a twisting trail, and we were not, just then,
prepared to travel that far.   However, a trail is a trail, easy
walking in the forest was what we were after, so why not let
the donkeys help?

Our clothes were soaked, water dripped from the turned-
down brims of our monte-cristis, and we felt almost cold.   The
black soil was well mixed with coarse volcanic sand and in places
puddled with water.   I could feel the sole of my right shoe
growing soft and thin, but I was enjoying my walk so much that
I could not worry about shoes.

As we moved along, single file like burros on the homeward
trail, I began to be aware of another version of the "Santiago
feeling," experienced only in the rain-forest of the mountains—
a feeling that we were in a friendlier presence than the pervading
spirit of the dry *playas*.   The forest closed us in, we could not
see the lava—full as it was of dormant menace—or the burned-
out craters or the empty ocean.   Here we saw nothing but
leafy, dripping trees hung with moss, earth and puddles of water
underfoot, and rain.   While these too were strange, being part
of a far-off, virgin place, they were also warmly friendly and
responsive—perhaps even kind.   The awe that I felt on the
playa and on the lava was lost in this wet, green forest.

Even before we had left the lava we had heard the finches
singing—thousands and thousands of tree-finches—though I do
not remember seeing one.   Their monotonous, endlessly repeated
notes—"Cher-níng, cher-níng, cher-níng," they said—and the
changeless and steady rustle of the rain seemed to time our footsteps and our very pulse beats, and I could imagine that as long
as the finches sang and the raindrops fell we could walk on
for ever and never grow tired.

We had followed the trail for the better part of an hour when

it turned to the east, away from the lava and deeper into the
forest.   The undergrowth was scanty, in many places not there
at all, for the large trees shut out too much of the light and few
plants could flourish under them.   Generally the forest remained
changeless—still many large nameless trees and those slim, pale-
stemmed strangers that stood up so straight and promised such
excellent building wood.   The rest were mostly *palos santos*—or
their first cousins.   These specimens were much larger than those
of the plain—the moisture in the mountains and the good black
soil would account for that difference—and they also had a
somewhat different leaf and a sweeter, spicier aroma, which
reminded me of licorice.

Now and then we came upon old friends.   *Espinos*—super-
thorne trees which Ainslie had often combated with his machete
on Floreana—*muyuyus de arriba*, and, in the more open places,
rodilla de cavallo blooming profusely and fragrantly.   The flowers
were pinkish-white and small, but grew in fair-sized clusters.
On the ground, occasionally, nettles and a species of "wandering
jew," which made me vaguely homesick.

Ainslie had hoped that the trail would swing back northward,
but after another half-hour we could see that it would not turn
soon enough.   There was a long way now between us and El
Corral, and we had to remember the road back.   We would have
to return along the trail to the Crater of the Fallen Trees or
take off through trailless terrain straight for the lava flow.
(I could have cursed the lava flow, but this forest did not seem
to be the proper place for curses.)

If the choice had been mine, I could not have chosen the
right direction—all directions to me were quite alike.   But
Ainslie knew—he always knows where he is headed, partly
through observation and partly through experience and a natural
gift.   I followed him confidently in the direction he said was west.

As soon as we had left the trail we found the jungle much
thicker, and, as we should have expected, immediately crossed
trails with a large herd of hogs.   Here then were the marks of
paradise as our friend Alfredo had seen them—"Here a pig,
there a pig, under every tree a pig!"   Well, paradise could have
done worse—these were fine hogs, not at all like their big-
headed, skimpy-rumped cousins of the plain, which, Ainslie said,
"wore their ears in the middle of their backs."   The hogs now
before our eyes were long in the back and thick in the hams,
and the boars seemed to carry a good thirty pounds of fat bacon
on their flanks.   The dozen sows were leaner, though with

extensive udders, and several of them were trailed by eight or ten fat, saucy-nosed piglets.

These animals were not at all afraid—they did not even look at us or the dog. They had probably never heard a gun fired or a dog barking. I wondered what these upland hogs ate to keep them fat—roots and grass alone seemed too thin a diet to make lard. Perhaps some of the trees bore nuts or fruit, though we had observed none on the trees we had seen. The two avocado trees reported present in these mountains could not have produced sufficient fruit to fatten hundreds, even thousands, of hogs.

Goats too were present in great numbers, very much like the *playa* animals. Goats often crossed the lava, but these must have remained in the uplands long enough to take on a more lush appearance. It was not likely that hogs ever crossed the flow, though they could have gone around it at the upper end. They probably spent their lives in the close vicinity of the place where they were born.

We walked a long time, longer than we had counted on, before we saw signs that the lava flow was near. The first sign was a ten-foot ridge of old, decayed lava covered with grey and green lichen and moss. We followed it northward, looking for an opening, but none appeared. "Climb it we must," said Ainslie, and climb it we did—I needed a little pushing—and we were not pleasantly surprised by what we found on the other side. A wide stretch of very rough, boulder-strewn ground— old, crumbled lava this too—further encumbered by trees and thorny shrubs.

A quarter of an hour later we were back on the solid black flow, far down toward the beach where the flow widens out. Just above the place where we would cross was an island of green trees—*palos santos*, mostly—a spot where the ground had been too high for the new lava to cover up. Ten thousand finches sang "Cher-níng, cher-níng, cher-níng" and "Quink, quink, quink, quink, quink," among the leafy branches and never seemed to stop. This island made it necessary to curve out a little, for we figured that crossing it would be difficult—too much broken-up, old lava and tangled vegetation. Next to the beach, almost opposite the island, were twin outcroppings of red slag—they looked like ruins of buildings. These ruins would hinder our passage not at all, for we had no need, at present, to go near them. We looked upon them as decoration and something to indicate what the newer flow had covered up.

I could never stop wondering what was under the lava—some old lava and slag, certainly, but also, very likely, a good stretch of the Pleasant Belt. Perhaps there had been springs here, or at least one spring—that did not seem too unreasonable to imagine, considering the nearness of the rainy mountains.

"Could be," I said, "that there's a grave under all this monstrous weight of black tombstone—even a grave once marked 'U.S.A.'!"

"You mean Lieutenant Cowan's grave, I suppose," Ainslie said.

"Yes. This lava was not here in 1913, you know. Perhaps that was why Captain Porter liked James Bay."

"Hadn't thought of that, but could be so." Ainslie was silent while we skirted around a buckle in the lava. Then he added: "What a time that guy will have getting out on Judgment Day!"

I was not so much concerned about Lieutenant Cowan on Judgment Day as I was about the hypothetical springs and the hypothetical fair valley. Why could we not have been at James Bay a hundred years ago, and more, when there was no raw

I

lava flow, no donkeys, goats, or pigs, and no nation whatever owned the island? And there must have been considerable water, for Captain Porter and the pirates before him had spent much time at James Bay. Why had the earth chosen just this place to spew out her flaming entrails—why not far out to sea, or some island like Marchena or Pinta, where the Conways did not care to live?

We had come to a smooth place on the lava, and Ainslie said: "This looks like a good spot to catch our breaths and sample the water."

I was glad enough to sit down. We were not thirsty, though neither of us had touched water for six hours and had been walking all that time. Nor were we hungry, though I now thought of food. "Do you know," I asked, "that we have not eaten since yesterday?"

"I am almost able to remember," Ainslie answered. "But how are your shoes making it?"

For an hour I had felt as if only my sock stood between me and whatever lay underfoot. I took off my right shoe and found a two-inch hole in the middle of the sole and the sock was all but worn through. I eased the difficulty by putting my left sock and one of Ainslie's under the torn sole and resolving to let the heel carry most of my weight. Three-fourths of the width of the lava remained to be traversed, but I was now fairly confident that I and what was left of the shoe could make it.

We sat facing the wooded slopes so recently left—they seemed very remote already because they were so different from the place we occupied at the moment and the sandstone flat to which we would soon return. Rain was still falling on them.

Just then I realised that our clothes were dry. "Do you remember when we got out of the rain?" I asked.

"Not exactly, but I think it was before we climbed over that moss-grown ridge."

"I think I know now what we ought to call those mountains."

"Okay. Name them."

"The Just and the Unjust Mountains."

"But that's a heck of a name—oh, I see, though. Because the rain falls alike on the just and the unjust. Far-fetched and cumbersome—still, I think I approve of it."

Paradise had been seen and its mountains named, and I felt a sense of accomplishment. "It has not been a bad day," I said.

"No, it has been a good day, and one we won't soon forget. But not yet ended. There's more lava to cross."

"And nothing for it but to cross it." I got up, determined to do or die.

We had to go around some very wide crevices and awesome buckles, but otherwise the second crossing was easier than the first. There were no bubbles and none of the crushed-glass formation, and we made better time—sixty minutes sufficed us to reach the other side.

This time we entered the sandstone country below the salt crater, and so were unable to pick any more plums from Santiago's lone, beat-up plum tree. "We'll go again day after tomorrow," I promised myself. "Tomorrow we'll probably be too tired."

At four o'clock we entered El Corral—our walk had used up nine hours. Considering everything—and everything included the cooking and eating of a whopping big dinner—we were not ashamed of ourselves that evening.

MANY things in the Galápagos are unique and unpredictable, but the seasonal changes are about as settled in their courses as they are anywhere else. However, they are settled in their own special Galápagos courses, which makes them worth describing.

If the climate of the islands were determined only by their location on the equator, the Galápagos would be a tropical region, hot and humid. But up from the Antarctic and along the western coast of the South American continent flows an immense, cold ocean river known as the Humboldt Current. This stream turns westward at the equator, washes and eddies about the bristling shores of the Enchanted Islands, then loses itself somewhere in the Pacific. In passing it makes the climate of the islands like no climate elsewhere. In no other place that we know of can you find two distinct climates running simultaneously only two miles apart.

Though, generally speaking, the islands have two seasons—the season of Capricorn and the season of Cancer—the close observer can distinguish five: spring, summer, autumn, and two phases of an anomalous season which we choose to call "pure Galápagan." The first three correspond pretty closely to the same seasons almost anywhere, except that they are much shorter, but the last "double" season probably has no counterpart.

The refrigerating action of the low ocean temperatures as well as the direction of the south-east trade winds, which blow from the Antarctic regions during the long south-polar winter, result not only in unexpectedly temperate thermometer readings —ranging roughly from 6o to 7o degrees Fahrenheit—but also in the eight or nine months' dry season of the low shore areas. The generous humidity that the south-east trade wind carry fails to condense and fall on the lowlands because the shore temperature is higher than that of the ocean. The moisture does condense, however, in the higher altitudes and comes down as mist and semi-perpetual drizzle on the mountains. The result is that in many places in the Galápagos one can travel from desert to rain-forest in half an hour.

During the Antarctic summer, which in Ecuador is called

winter, after the northern fashion, the Humboldt is warmer and deviates somewhat from its usual course. Then the islands have a tropical climate, and the temperature often reaches 95 degrees Fahrenheit or more and rains are general on both highlands and lowlands—heavy, sudden showers of the typical equatorial variety. It is during this season of Capricorn that the variations corresponding to spring, summer and fall can be observed.

From the time of our arrival on Santiago early in December until the middle of January we slept under heavy woollen blankets, hand-woven by Quechua women in the ten-thousand-foot Andean altitudes. The nights were that cool. And though the sun was hot and brilliant, the daytime air temperature was very comfortable. We shivered while taking our salt-water baths in the tide pools and ate our six o'clock dinner wearing coats. We were still enjoying the tail-end of the pure Galápagan season.

The wind blew freshly and steadily from the south-east, though by January it had begun to vary a little, taking a turn from the west or north occasionally. At night it usually went down completely, but by eight in the morning it was up and at it again. Each variation in the wind brought other rain signs— "mackerel scales and mares' tails" and heavy cloud masses on the northern horizon.

Occasionally, as if in answer to our prayers—prayers which we redeemed from over-seriousness by irreverent words—it did rain a little. This happened generally at night or in the late morning. A little cap of mist would appear on Sugar Loaf, and as we watched, crossing our fingers and saying "That piffling cloud is too small to do us any good," just by way of teasing contrary Nature into some thoughtless and unusual action, the cloud would grow larger and spread out toward our territory. Usually we could see it dropping its moisture on the mountain, over the area of the spring and half-way to El Corral, then the cloud would move away across the lava or to the west where it was dissipated over the ocean. Now and then it reached far enough our way to hang a few minutes over El Corral and give us a couple of buckets of fresh water off the metal roof. We called these "two-bucket rains." Our first four-bucket rain was a big event.

Up in the mountains, even at this season, we could see that it rained almost daily for several hours. Sunlight from our side against the heavy clouds made many rainbows—there was scarcely a day without at least one. Sometimes they were only

fragments of bows or shapeless spots of iridescence that formed
and faded and formed again.   At other times perfect half-circles
appeared, with perhaps one end on the lava and the other in
the ocean.   These were often double bows—the second one a
paler mirror-image of the first.

This changing season gave us a sense of spring.   The
showers, though skimpy, were fresh and had a feeling of newness.
The apparently dead flatland vegetation began showing signs of
life and the animals too responded to the more stimulating
surroundings.

Our *palo santo* trees, which always lose their leaves during
the season of Cancer whether it is wet or dry, had already been
budding when we arrived.   By the end of January they were
well leafed-out in delicate bright green and heavily hung with
droopy clusters of greenish blossoms.   Their aroma was all per-
vasive at this stage, though having it in our nostrils constantly
made us all but unaware of it.

The *muyuyus* and *aromos,* which never shed all their leaves
unless extreme drought forces them into it, also began to change
their dusty old clothes for bright new ones.   The yellow *muyuyu*
blossoms, growing in clusters of from two to six, were an inch
in diameter but with no fragrance.   They had a habit of falling,
unwithered, and lying on the ground tossed around by the wind
without perceptible change.   The *aromos* put on thousands of
little deliciously fragrant flowers, like fluffy yellow powder-puffs.
It seemed odd that a tree so gnarled and thorny should bear
such delicate lacy leaves and such delicate blossoms.   Yet Nature
had shown wisdom in creating it so, for the flowers and leaves
were edible to all vegetarian animals of Santiago and without
the protection of thorns the trees would not have survived.

When the sun was directly overhead we noted with particular
gratitude a certain habit of the *aromo* trees.   Their leaves folded
up tightly at night and whenever it rained, but the hotter and
brighter the sun, the more wakefully they spread their dainty
leaves to catch the burning rays.   The result was that we had
good shade in our *patio*.   Had the *aromos* folded up their leaves
in the heat of midday, as some trees do, we would have had
to move our camp to the shade of the *palos santos* on Pirate
Flat.

On the sandstone flats grew a small plant which must have
been a variety of the so-called "resurrection plant."   During the
dry periods, under the bright sun, it seemed quite dead, the leaves
spreading grey and flat from the centre of growth.   But after

each shower, even a one-bucket sprinkle, the leaves turned dark green—they were purple on the under side—and tiny white eyes of blossoms opened. As soon as the sun came out and the plant dried, it changed to grey again and the flowers disappeared.

After a couple of half-barrel rains at the end of January, the entire island turned green. Grass and weeds sprouted on every bit of soil and even in places where, to our eyes, there was no soil. Little *aromos*, morning glories, and ground cherries pushed up through our kitchen floor. New growth shoots appeared on stringy, beat-up, goat-nibbled bushes we had thought dead. Even the thorn bushes, which could not have become any greener (for greenness was their natural state under all conditions as long as they were alive), expanded some of their thorns into more leaflike shapes. And as the leaves came on, the last of the berries ripened quickly and fell off, depriving the doves, finches, and me of our daily fruit ration. But, as though in compensation, the struggling plants in my garden dots stretched and expanded, promising fruitfulness.

Every living thing was in a hurry to breed at this season. Mocking-birds, finches, and flycatchers had young in nests all around us. Lizards laid their eggs in holes they dug in the earth, all our donkeys carried extended bellies, and the three hens laid and clucked and laid again. Doves and hawks were absent from the flatlands—they must have been nesting elsewhere. Flies, grasshoppers, moths, and all other insects multiplied. The same sort of activity was probably at its height in the now warmed-up depths of the ocean.

One pair of yellow-breasted flycatchers was especially frantic. One day Ainslie happened to throw a piece of sacking on a limb in such a way as to form a loop, and before he had his hand off the burlap a flycatcher had deposited a twig in the loop. A second later his mate had dropped in a feather. There were three days of hectic action, bringing in bedding and, between trips, snapping up flies and moths to keep the hard-working little engines fuelled up. Within a week the nest contained four eggs—tiny white jewels scarcely bigger than peas.

February brought us heavy heat and really heavy rains. The effect of both heat and rain was made worse for us by the location of our camping spot. Though El Corral was very pleasant and suitable in the dry, cool season, during the tropical months it was a little inferno. We got the heat doubled—from the sun above and from the sandstone walls, which absorbed the sun's heat and reflected it back. The walls also cut off the breeze, and the sod-buster downpours made a muddy torrent of the gully bottom.

Our worst rain came early in March. Fortunately it came in the daytime, when we could keep an eye on it. It started at two o'clock, as a perfect shower, which filled our two rain-tanks exactly to the rim and then stopped. "A rain made to order," Ainslie rejoiced. "Could anything have been neater?"

At three heavy clouds formed again. They did not come from anywhere in particular—they just made themselves out of the saturated air right over our heads and all around us. We seemed to be the nucleus of an immense, black cloud mass.

There were sharp flashes of lightning—not at a distance, but right *there*—and tremendous crashes of thunder that made our tin roof vibrate like a tuning fork. Then the clouds turned to water. We were in the centre of a cloud as it "burst."

A great muddy stream was soon surging through and over the back entrance of El Corral, regardless of the stones blocking it, washing around the house, flooding the *patio* floor, and escaping through the front gate, where it joined a still greater stream from the west fork of the canyon. United, the two streams rioted through the "front yard," around and over the garden dots, under the chicken-roost trees, and on into the ocean, carrying with them a rich load of precious loam, dry sticks, and flood-loosened weeds and grass.

The fire steamed and hissed as it went out, though we had covered it with a piece of metal, shaped into a "gable roof," which was the rain cap that ordinarily protected the fireplace well enough. We sat on our beds where we had pulled them into the middle of the shelter area, but even there we could not keep dry. The wind blew in in splashes of water as it changed direction at each moment and the air was filled with a thick, eddying drizzle. This went on for two hours. For some reason the hours seemed short, though we did not try to divert ourselves by reading or doing anything else except watching and marvelling.

As darkness approached we began to worry about dinner, for no cooking was possible as long as the rain lasted. We had cold stew in plenty and crackers, but now when getting it seemed impossible, we developed a powerful yearning for hot tea. We also wondered what happened to the birds in weather like this. Wouldn't the nestlings drown? Our own chickens were up in their tree, no doubt, soaked, limp and ragged. Then I remembered the yellow hen tied to the trunk of a tree which now stood

in the torrent washing into the bay. I had put her there that
morning, giving her a six-foot string, to break her of a brooding
spell.

"She's drowned for certain," I said to Ainslie.

"Too late to worry now," he said. "And if she is not dead,
she is certainly 'cooled off'."

Toward six o'clock the rain slackened, and we waded out
to rescue the hen, if she was still in rescuable shape, and to see
how much damage the deluge had done.

Under the chicken *muyuyu* was a natural depression and this·
now contained a pool about three feet deep. We stirred with
sticks where the hen ought to have been but brought up no
sign of her. Ainslie glanced up among the dripping branches,
where it was already dark, and saw what looked like a bundle of
wet gunny-sacking hanging on a string. This proved to be our
hen. Evidently she had tried to fly up into the tree, the string
had caught on a limb, and there she hung, head downward, by
one foot. Water was still running from the end of her bill.
Ainslie shook some of the water from her feathers and she
squawked feebly. We wanted to dry her out, but having no
fire, we wrapped her in a sack and put her under a box to recover
or die.

Back on the beach, we saw that a great, ugly gash had been
washed through the sand, and at the Goya Rico Beach the gash
was even uglier. The bay was muddy for half a mile out, and
dead brush and even good-sized tree trunks floated in it. It
hurt us to see the best topsoil of the island going to waste in the
sea. Most of the brush that had previously choked up the
gullies and held back the silt had died during the dry years. On
the sandstone flats that surrounded us there had never been
enough vegetation to hold back the surface flow after a rain
like this.

Darkness came while we stood there deploring—especially
heavy darkness that night, for the clouds still hung low and the
wet sandstone and lava were much darker than when dry. We
returned to El Corral and decided not to light a fire. The
attempt would have been useless. The wood and the fireplace
were thoroughly soaked, and the post deluge rain kept on falling.
We ate cold stew and fudge and called them good. Bed and
blankets were good too, for we were wet and chilled.

I woke next morning to a soft knocking sound. Half asleep,
I was about to say: "Wait till I get some clothes on and I'll open
the door." Then remembering that we had no door, I sat up

and listened. That knocking again. Just like a hen pecking a board—which was exactly the right comparison. The yellow hen had managed to revive and was pecking on the box to be let out. She ate the corn I gave her but refused water. Her experience had left no mark on her, except that she did not have another brooding spell for six weeks.

We had hoped that the rain would soak the soil to a depth of at least three feet. In some places this happened, as under the chicken *muyuyus,* where a three-foot stand of water seeped into the earth, but in our living area and in the other gullies the soil was wet only a couple of inches—in some spots not that much. The water had come down with such force and the earth had been so dry that the topsoil was washed away as fast as it was moistened. All we could count on as gain from our cloudburst was more water in the spring. If our estimate was correct, all the craters on the island, including Sugar Loaf, should have been well-filled storage basins now.

The improvement in our spring-water supply was not immediate. That day, when Ainslie returned from the spring unusually late, his face was bleak. His hard-won water-hole had been filled up with silt. Sand, old bones, dead wood, and even boulders had choked the bottom of the spring canyon, and half of the garden terrace had been washed away. A good two weeks' work would be necessary to clean up the spring and repair the damage.

Repairs were necessary in the home area too. The *patio* floor had to be shovelled out, the little terraced garden back of the house had to be built up again with higher and stronger retaining walls. A new trail had to be carved out of the canyon side toward the beach, for the water had washed out a ledge which had formed part of our trail. And Ainslie was not satisfied with mere repairs—he made improvements. With the pick he dug a ditch in the sandstone above El Corral to divert water from our house canyon into another farther off. This meant days of toil in the scorching sun, but, in Ainslie's opinion, the expected results were worth the effort and suffering.

One pleasant task we had and we perfromed it with proper ceremony. The "O.K. BUT LITTLE WATER HERE NOW" sign seemed too silly in our present circumstances. Perhaps it had always been silly. No sky-rider, unless it be an angel, had come to read it in the four months we had now spent on the island. While I watched, Ainslie piled up neatly and separately all the pieces of pottery that had made each letter, so that the result would have appeared like a row of dots to an airman. We left them that way for some chance visitor to puzzle over.

March brought us the culmination of all hot-season evils. In February we had yearned for March "to get it over with," and in March we yearned for April, for then the heat would begin to abate. But only begin. Not until May could we hope for real improvement.

During the worst months I formed the habit of wearing wet clothes—I found that a wet shirt and slacks were cooler than dry shorts and a halter or nothing at all. I made the first wetting about ten o'clock in the morning and, as fast as my clothes dried, I wet them again until around five in the afternoon. Ainslie depended on semi-nakedness and sweat to keep him in comfort, and even he stayed in the shade during the hottest hours of the afternoon. At night we slept "raw" under a thin sheet and a canopy of mosquito netting.

The heat was *that* bad only in our gully and other similar gullies in the lowlands. On many a March evening, when we went on one of the near-by hills to catch the breeze and take our nightly look-around over the island and the ocean, we planned to bring our beds up there the next evening. But we never did it, for the task of rigging up the mosquito nets, though not really difficult, always seemed too much trouble. Perhaps, in spite of the heat, we found some comfort in sleeping under our familiar roof, surrounded by our fortress walls. Too much solitude in these wide, wilderness spaces was giving us a touch of agoraphobia.

The combination of heat and blinding sunlight was good for one thing. Some of the weevils that had infested the corn had got into the rice and were multiplying fast indeed. On a day when the heat waves were boiling up from the black sand in our front yard so alarmingly that I imagined I smelt sulphur fumes, I spread all the remaining rice on sheets of metal on the ground.

"You'll get sunstroke out there," Ainslie objected.

"You are going to dig and shovel and carry rocks in the sun yourself," I reminded him. "What about your getting sunstroke?"

"I don't. I'm immune."

"Anyhow, I don't expect to stand out there and watch the *bichos* die. I'll be satisfied just to view the remains."

An hour later, well shaded by my wide hat and wearing

sun-glasses, I went to see how the weevils were doing. The rice was hot on my fingers as I stirred it, while the scorching earth burned my feet through my shoes and the sun held a living flame three feet from my back. I found all the weevils huddled at the bottom against the metal, which also burned my fingers. I poked at the *bichos* and they made a brittle-dry sound. Not even a miracle could ever bring them to life again.

It was doubly difficult now to keep fresh or cooked food from spoiling before we could eat it up. I tried to cook in small quantities, but this was not always possible in our system of economy. A large kettleful of soup cooked before noon was still hot enough to eat at six in the evening. If soup or stew was to be kept for more than one day, I let it boil at least ten minutes both morning and evening. At this season we always cooked our fish within an hour after it was caught and never tried to keep it from one meal to the next.

Everything grew fast, matured fast, went to seed fast, as if in a hurry to get its life cycle finished before the drought caught it. But grass put on trillions of prickly seed pods, which caught in our clothes and our hair, and even sneaked into our beds. We could have cursed it, but we did not. During our first stay on Santiago we had made a roof of bur-grass, having no other roofing materials, and lived under it three months. After all, we had some feelings of gratitude.

May came—finally, the rains ceased, and the cool south-east trades were back on the job. The change brought with it souvenirs and suggestions of autumns we had known. The grass and weeds turned brown, the *palo santo* leaves darkened and fell off. The caterpillars disappeared from the *muyuyus* and *aromos,* where they had annoyed us all summer. Flies and mosquitoes thinned out as tourists thin out from a popular resort in September. The hawks and doves, which had been summering in the mountains, came back to the beaches. By mid-June the weather and the island were about as they had been in mid-December, and the welcome "pure Galápagan" season was with us again.

XII. OUR SOCIAL CIRCLE OR KNEE-DEEP IN LIZARDS

Social prestige is generally based on culture, wealth, doughty deeds, or time spent in a place. In the case of the Santiago inhabitants, culture was pretty hard to evaluate. The Conways had the most of such culture as the human world considers prestige-worthy. But since we could not tell for sure if this sort of refinement was of any value on Santiago, we could not use it as a touchstone. Wealth was out too, for none of the islanders had any. Nor could we judge social rank by deeds, not because they were of doubtful value but because we could not decide just what deeds carried the most weight. I might have given myself an A for living months on end without seeing a woman's face, except when I was shocked by my own in a mirror about once a week. Ainslie might have earned a high mark for "carrying the cross" or driving a couple of wild goats home like a team of trotting horses. But were these mightier than the deeds of the goats themselves when they took refuge on foot-wide ledges that overhung thirty feet of sheer cliff below which the breakers raged? Or the derring-do of mocking-birds when they crippled or killed each other in fights over nesting-places? Time spent on the island was the only criterion that would serve us—the oldest in lineage and holdings would have to be the aristocrats.

The viruses, the bacteria, and the germs came first. But since we had no microscope except a little water-drop affair Ainslie had made himself we could not become familiar with them. Some of them helped ferment my rice beer or made neglected soup whisper. Others were not present—bacilli of tuberculosis, malarial organisms, or similar first families. On the whole, a group out of our class.

Some of the very oldest inhabitants were no doubt in the sea. Ainslie caught enough sharks to develop a great respect for them, for they had "been around" quite a while, some two hundred million years maybe. But old-timers or not, they had the misfortune to live beyond the "pale," which was the shoreline of our island.

We were in some trouble deciding whether to include the creatures of the shore—such as sea iguanas, crabs—and seabirds in our register, for society seldom takes note of borderline populations—those who live neither on Nob Hill nor South of Market, but somewhere between or in the suburbs. We compromised by including some of them in our set and ignoring the others. Social arbiters must draw arbitrary lines, though sometimes rather crooked ones.

Which then, of those we meant to recognise and receive, should we place at the head of the table? Are insects older than reptiles? How old are centipedes? Which came first, the spider or the fly? No clear answer. We cut the knot and gave the crown to the reptiles.

And among the reptiles, which first? The giant tortoises, or galápagos, of course. They had given their name to the islands. They had been glamorised, publicised, immortalised—perhaps would, when they were all dead, be sanctified, and the islands of their name would be called Santos Galápagos. These beasts were already so rare on Santiago that we never saw one, though we may have seen some fossilised eggs—if they were galápagos eggs and not land iguana eggs. (Ainslie found the eggs some three feet below the surface of the earth when he was improving the road to the spring. There were dozens of the fossilised shells, mostly in fragments, originally spherical and about two inches in diameter.) We have seen photographs of Santiago galápagos taken twelve years ago. The reptiles probably still exist on the island if those boorish upstarts, the domestic-hogs-gone-wild, have not finished their line by devouring all the eggs and young.

The second most representative Galápagos creatures are the iguanas. According to Darwin, there were so many land iguanas on Santiago a hundred years ago that the scientist's party could scarcely find tent-space on ground that was not pitted with iguana holes. To our knowledge there are no land iguanas left on Santiago, certainly not in the James Bay region. The south and east sides of the island have not been explored, and, as far as anyone knows, almost anything could exist there—even the giant *iguanón* the Ecuadorian sailors told us about. The *iguanón*, they said, was as large as a dinosaur and extremely ferocious.

Sea iguanas are still present and not so much in danger of extinction. They are similar to land iguanas—lizardlike creatures which attain a length of four feet or so—but black or a very dark lava grey all over instead of being marked with yellow, orange,

blue, and other colours as are the land iguanas. They feed on
seaweed and spend most of their lives on tide-washed rocks. If
an enemy approaches from land, they jump into the surf, if from
the sea, they climb on the rocks. Though they look like horrific
black dragons, they are timid and harmless.

Having now made a polite bow to the big shots among the
reptiles, or their shades, we now become downright chummy
with the little shots. The Santiago family of lizards, members of
which also inhabit most of the other islands of the group, are
charming creatures, as all friendly small creatures are charming.
Sometimes we ate out of the same dishes and slept in the same
beds with them.

Everywhere in the dry areas of the James Bay region these
lizards were always underfoot, but more than a chance number
seemed to inhabit El Corral. If we were away from the *patio* an
hour, lizard tracks obliterated all other tracks, including our own.
Sometimes, in irritable moods, we complained that we were
wading knee-deep in lizards. They were probably attracted by
the nice niches in the tufa fence and in the fireplace and by the
flies and other edibles that were more abundant in our kitchen
than elsewhere in the vicinity. We learned to know them not
only *en masse* but as individuals. As social individuals, that is,
not specimens, for we are not biologists—which is a pity.

The adult males of the species reach a length of six inches or
more. They are generally grey on the back or a sort of tweedy
mixture with red, green, yellow, and white markings on the sides
and the head. The females, which are considerably smaller, are
greyish brown with a scarlet throat. These colours varied somewhat in individuals—once we saw a young male with a definitely
green back. Their rough, dry skins blended perfectly with the
greys, browns, and greens of their surroundings. Decoratively
speaking, they were becoming to El Corral.

The lizards lived chiefly on flies and other insects, but they
would also take bits of meat, cooked rice, soup, an occasional
scorpion, and, we suspected, a piece of lizard now and then.
One young male who inhabited the fireplace and spent some of
the best months of his life scurrying about or lying on the warm
top stones habitually picked up whatever food particles I happened to drop while cooking, from fried goat liver to sugar
syrup. Ainslie always fed the scorpions he killed to his pet
lizards.

At first we did not welcome so many lizards in our household,
but after a few weeks of living with them we did not wish one

of them away. A cleaner, less troublesome multitude of pets
could not have been found. They left no slimy trails, no soil
or residue of any kind, and surely no germs, as some pets might
have done. Their sun-baked bodies were thoroughly sanitary.
If we did not learn to love them—a reptile is difficult to love—we
did definitely like them.

They were entertaining, too, as well as useful. They raced
and fought and bobbed and bowed—evidently they were beautifully "adjusted" and enjoyed life. And when they darted up
our bare legs or backs, they did it to liquidate a molesting fly.
If they ran up a table leg and flicked a lightning tongue toward
the meat on our plates, that too helped us as well as them—each
flick meant one less fly.

The most interesting of our little housemates was a female
who had lost her right front leg and her tail. How she had lost
the leg we could not guess, but the missing tail was easy to
explain. There were others without tails, and I had seen one
of them lose his end-piece. He got into a fight with a larger
male, and the two of them wrestled and ju-jitsued and slapped
each other with their tails. The smaller lizard, realising he was
getting the worst of it, broke lose and started to run. The
other caught him by the tail and the tail came off.

The loss of a lizard's tail is not a great calamity. He grows
a new one, as the little female was in the process of doing, though
the second tail never seems to grow as large as the first. The
loss of a leg, however, is not so trifling. Legs cannot be replaced,
though Left-legged Lizzie, as we called her, could run fast enough
on her remaining three, with a sort of diagonal movement.

In addition to being only a fraction, Lizzie had two other
characteristics that set her apart from other lizards: she was so
tame that we could pick her up any time and she had an exceptionally cold belly.

Each morning, after a cool night, we noticed that all our
lizards liked to warm their bellies on sun-warmed rocks. Lizzie
was so cold—or so smart—that she did not wait for the sun
to warm a rock for her. As soon as we had a fire lighted she
climbed on the rocks next to the fire bed and spread herself out.
Sometimes, even when I was sweating and steaming, Lizzie was
on the hot stones. She liked to be warm, and nature had not
provided her with a central-heating system.

During the hot season, when every creature was breeding
furiously, Lizzie kept well up with the others. Her belly was
fat with eggs, not only once but, it seemed to me, a half-dozen

times. After she had kitty-cornered about like a blown-up balloon for a few days, she dug a hole, backed herself into it until only her head and one front leg showed, and stayed so for a while—perhaps fifteen minutes, perhaps an hour. Then she came out, her belly slender, and covered up the hole. For a few days she guarded the hole, aided by a large, handsome male, and then seemed to forget about it. If any little lizards hatched, we did not see them. Yet some lizards must have hatched in the thousands of nests on the island.

The lizards were daytime creatures, but their cousins, the geckos, moved about only at night. They were less than three inches long, mottled with shades of grey, and had large black eyes and little knobs, or suction cups, on the ends of their toes. I found them in the packing-boxes and behind the dishes in the cupboard, and when they were discovered they searched desperately for another dark place to hide. There was something pathetic and helpless about them. We never molested them, if we could avoid it, for they ate scorpions and other vermin which were less welcome among the teacups. Sometimes I heard them

K

at night, making little chirring noises, though Ainslie's hearing was not keen enough to catch their kind of music.

A three-foot snake lived among our fireplace stones, though we seldom saw him; he was very shy as well as quite harmless. One day when I had had a hot fire going for several hours he came out—probably because his hide-out got too warm. We were sitting at the table, eating, and in a panic the snake started up the table leg. Ainslie got up, horrified, but I was only interested in seeing if the snake could make it to the table-top. Before two-thirds of his length was against the leg he fell off and escaped into a crack in the fence.

Perhaps the centipedes were of a family more ancient than the reptiles, but since they were not friendly or glamorous we wasted little attention on them. Ainslie found them under rocks when he was making the corral fence and he always cut them in at least four pieces, for each of them seemed to have at least two lives. (Once I found a centipede under Ainslie's pillow when I was making up the bed and I cut him in two with a butcher's knife. Each half ran away, in opposite directions.) We admitted that we might be wrong in killing centipedes—perhaps they ate insects and otherwise made themselves useful in the balance of nature. However, we had been told that centipedes bite, or sting, and are poisonous, so there seemed to be sufficient excuse for liquidating those we found in El Corral. There were still plenty and more left on the island to keep their line unbroken. Incidentally, looked at from the point of view of æsthetics, they were beautiful—some five inches long and of a shiny reddish-brown colour.

We could not possibly take note of all the spiders and insects and their relatives—there were so many of them that even a trained biologist could have spent months studying them. There were at least six species of mere flies, and it is not likely that we counted all of them, and many more kinds of moths. In the interest of self-defence we could not ignore some of them, however, and others were colourful enough in appearance or habits to attract our notice.

In any society the individuals with stings get special consideration—they are either appeased or liquidated. We never put our hand into a packing-box or the dish-cupboard or our foot into a shoe without first investigating them for the presence of scorpions. That is, we observed the precaution after each of us had been stung once. The sting was jolting, something like a bee sting raised to the third power. We always killed scorpions and doing it was not always easy. One extra large one which had snuggled between the sheets in my bed was about to escape, and in my haste I reached for the Flit gun. I soaked him well, but he kept on running. The next nearest weapon was the machete, but I only managed to cut off his tail before he hid under a slab of sandstone. He may have lived, but I doubt that he ever stung again.

Among the more distant spider relatives, the hermit crabs were the best mixers socially. The red Sally Lightfoots that decorated the shore, the almost invisible black crabs, the fiddler crabs, and the lobsters were all good enough from the biologist's point of view, but they had to be sought out. The hermits, belying their name, were willing to call on us at any time, though they preferred the dark hours. Every morning, when we got up, the soft mixture of sand and dust which made the *patio* floor was thoroughly stencilled with the tracks of hermit crabs—mixed, of course, with the spoor of lizards, geckos, birds, ant lions, and an occasional rat or mouse. These crabs climbed trees; one made a habit of sleeping daily in the branches of a bush beside our front gate. Others preferred to sleep in hens' nests; the yellow hen sat on one for two days, mistaking it for an egg.

The rat trap, which we kept set at night near the wood-pile, just "in case," was sprung once in the middle of the night. When Ainslie got up to investigate he found nothing in it, but around it were scattered the fragments of a hermit crab's shell—borrowed shell, of course. The crab had probably escaped injury and scurried off, naked and shaken, to find himself another shell.

Among the troublesome insects the white termites were the most destructive. They ate the strings which held up our tomato vines, and one night during the hot season a colony moved into our bedroom and ate the bottom out of Ainslie's duffle bag and a six-inch patch from the canvas covering of my suitcase. Had there been enough of them they could have eaten us naked and houseless. Fortunately, they were timid and could not stand daylight, so that with vigilance they could be kept under control.

Flies and mosquitoes were annoying as they always are, but really bad only in the hot season. Large ants got into the sugar and little ants into the meat and fat, but there were not too many of either and they did not get into our beds and bite us as the Argentine ants of Floreana had done. Perhaps the Floreana ants were importations from the continent.

Some of our insects were extremely pretty, though, on the

whole, Galápagos insects are smaller and less colourful than corresponding species elsewhere. Of those wearing fancy costumes, the most numerous were the giant grasshoppers. They were always present in the dry areas, but in the hot season they could have been counted by the millions. When we walked out on the flats, they flew into our faces and got tangled in our hair. They were about three inches long and well daubed with green, red, and yellow on a black background. The chickens grew fat eating them. There is even good Biblical authority that grasshoppers are good human food, too, and sometimes when we tired of our monotonous diet we considered trying some fried, but could not quite summon sufficient courage.

Among our loveliest were the little moths whose green caterpillars ate the pumpkin and cucumber plants. They were three-quarters of an inch long and had pearly-pink wings bordered with maroon. Green lace-wing flies were graceful and delicate. Another insect beauty, a stranger to us and rare, we named the "tail-light fly." It looked like a cross between a small dragonfly and a moth and had black-and-white wings and a red hind-end. Butterflies, which are gaudy in most tropical regions, were not very notable on our island. We saw only a few yellow, white, and orange-and-black specimens.

Hawk moths of various kinds were numerous enough during the hot season and they laid their eggs on the *muyuyu* and *aromo* leaves, which resulted in thousands of caterpillars—black-and-gold ones on the *aromos* and large green ones on the *muyuyus*. Birds ate up most of the smaller larvæ, but even mocking-birds seldom fed on the big three-inchers.

The only bee we noticed was a fat, black bumble-bee. He seemed always busy and no doubt carried pumpkin pollen to the water-melons and cucumber pollen to the tomatoes. He was comfortable to have around, for he minded his own business and the drone of his flight was soothing and homelike.

Birds, the latest comers on the island scene—except immigrant foreigners, who don't count—we always had with us.

The seabirds and we had no common meeting ground; the interest we took in them they did not in any way return. Pelicans, boobies, shearwaters, gulls, frigate birds, and sea swallows were all equally indifferent. With the exception of the night heron, the shore birds were also unmindful of us. But even these self-sufficient creatures furnished us with entertainment and material for observation and occasionally were of some use—commercial use, of all things.

It was good spectator sport to watch the boobies dive and the frigate birds fly, activities in which they excelled. Better still was watching a pelican take a bath. Why birds which spend half their waking time, and perhaps sleeping time too, upon and in sea water should go to the trouble of taking a bath in the same was beyond us. They might, of course, have been getting rid of parasites. Boobies bathed too, though they were not nearly so funny about it, no doubt because they were not essentially comic creatures.

The pelicans rolled from side to side, now with one wing under, now the other, then ducked their heads, and finally immersed their entire bodies, with a good deal of flopping and splashing. When they were thoroughly wet they swam ashore and stood on the sand or rocks, legs spraddled and wings fanning, as they dried themselves out. When I saw one the first time in this position, I looked for a long time before I realised what I was looking at. For a while I thought a strange monster, quite unknown to me, or the biologists, had crawled out of the mysterious depths of the ocean.

The most beautiful of the seabirds was an occasional visitor to the islands and we never saw him except in flight. He was the tropic bird—shining white, with a black spot on each wing and two luminous white streamers for a tail. Against the pure blue of the Galápagos sky he was certainly from heaven.

The oyster catcher gull was a sort of brightly-painted bird robot. He was black, with a red bill, like two painted sticks, and yellow legs. We came upon him a few times while both he and we were walking on the beach. When alarmed he made a mechanical-sounding noise—"kik-kik, kik-kik"—which reminded me of castanets.

A shore bird and cousin to the night heron who liked to play on our roof was the blue heron, or the "Bird-who-follows-his-bill." He got the nickname because that was just what he did. He held his bill in a horizontal position at the level of his body and seemed to be boring a passage through the air. Most of his life was spent among the rocks of the shore, looking for little crabs and other edibles or dozing. A few times a couple of them poked about in El Corral, but did not seem to like it much. Once I came upon a young member of this species on the beach. I walked around him, watching him, and he walked around me, watching me. Finally, feeling a little embarrassed with all that circling and staring, I moved away slowly, not to frighten him, though I doubt that he would ever have been startled.

We had two other salt-water birds, though they cared nothing about the ocean—a small teal duck and a large rose-coloured flamingo. Usually they were at home in the crater lake and other salt pools, but during our present stay on the island we saw each of them only once. A visiting yachtsman brought us two dressed ducks, which he had shot in a salt pool near the lava flow, and on our last day on Santiago we saw a dozen flamingos in formation flight high over El Corral, which seemed to us ominous.

The list of Santiago land birds is not very long: two kinds of hawks, several species of finches, two or three species of fly-catchers, two species of warblers, mocking-birds, owls, doves— that is the lot. We had what might be called personal relations with only the hawks, doves, flycatchers, and mocking-birds, though during our first stay on the island we had been on cursing terms also with the finches. The latter are chiefly plantation pests, and this time we had no plantation to speak of.

Our dealings with these landlubbers were mostly incidental to other experiences, but the mocking-birds were an experience in themselves. There are, in any society, certain families or individuals that cannot be treated casually, no matter what their position on the ladder of social status. They are the "colourful" characters, and on our island these attention-holders were the mocking-birds.

There were four mockers' nests of varying age and repair in out *aromos*, and in two nests families of young were produced. The birds had been around since our arrival, but only at the beginning of the hot season did they show any interest in the nests. One pair claimed all of them and they fought off every other bird who acted as if he might be nest-hunting. They investigated each nest, made a few repairs on one, abandoned it, and worked on another. Finally they decided on a nest—not the best one in our opinion—and built it up with *aromo* thorns and grass.

While the eggs were being incubated and for weeks before and after, mocking-bird war was a daily and continuous affair. There was no mockery about these battles—sometimes they were so ferocious that our weak nerves could not take it, and one or the other of us stirred the tangled combatants with a stick until they let go and called it a truce for a few minutes. Often the fighters were so exhausted that they could not fly away but lay on the ground for a while, panting. There were no fights to the death among our *patio* birds, as far as we knew, but perhaps there would have been if we had not interfered.

In a week or so after hatching, the young ones—four in this first batch—made loud cheeping noises that even Ainslie could hear. "Eat, eat!" they seemed to say every two minutes. We could see them pop up their heads, which were only the flimsy framework of an immense mouth, whenever the hard-working parent birds appeared with insects.

Even while they were frantically busy feeding their young and protecting their holdings, the birds adhered to odd, apparently time-wasting habits. Our patience was short during the hot season, and we wanted to tell them to be more progressive like us North Americans and try a few labour-saving short cuts. The mocking-birds avoided flying whenever they could run and never made straight flights if it was possible to make a détour or a stop over somewhere. Yet they were capable of long straight flights, for we had seen them do it.

Once I saw a bird pick a caterpillar from the *muyuyu* tree that shaded the fireplace. In one flight of thirty feet he could have taken the worm directly to his nest. But no, that was not his way. He flew down on the ground, hopped on a branch, then on a higher one, and walked along it as far as he could go in the direction of the nest, flew on the ground again, and then into the tree which held his nest—but not straight to his objective even yet. He hopped from limb to limb until he was on the home stretch, then walked the rest of the way. He had spent ten times as much time and energy as he needed, though perhaps he had a reason. This could have been one of his ways to avoid giving away the location of the nest to an enemy—a senseless way, for meantime the nestlings were cheeping loud enough to be heard two hundred feet.

Many times a day, though oftenest toward evening, one of the birds made a habit of patrolling the corral wall. He would run along the smooth stones, lap after lap, as if this running had a serious purpose and had to be completed within a certain time or else. Yet he seemed to be having fun too, for now and then he stopped to hop excitedly and call or even sing a little. The distance around the corral was about ten rods and the bird must have run the better part of a mile each day just fence patrolling. He may have been letting his enemies know where his domain began and that he was on the job seeing that it continued to begin there.

When the young birds were ready to leave the nest, they simply left it without any preliminaries. One evening they were in the nest yelling "Eat, eat!" and the next sunrise they were running about the *patio* yelling "Eat, eat!" They looked just like what they were—children tumbled out of bed in their grey flannel pyjamas, their hair standing on end. For a couple of weeks these young ones made no effort to find their own food, but followed their parents, with their mouths wide open crying "Eat, eat!" We tried to feed them exactly the same stuff their parents gave them and also bits of meat and rice, but they accepted nothing from us, though we thought it likely that, if their parents had abandoned them at this point, they would have learned to eat out of our hands.

In our household, which, to be fair, was their household too, the fledglings acted like undisciplined children. They were curious about everything and they investigated everything. They were all over the place—the beds, the tables, the fireplace, the pans and kettles. They pecked at their reflections in the mirror, looked behind it to find that other fellow, and rattled the dishes in the cupboard. One day one of them pulled all the pins and needles out of my pin-cushion and scattered them on the ground.

We called all the young birds Ruthie and Pete because those were the nearest approach in English to the calls their parents made most frequently. We did not know which were really Ruthies and which Petes, but that did not seem to matter.

The youngsters did not change their ways much as they matured, for their baby manners were little different from adult mocker manners. They learned eventually to get their own food— they had to, for the parent birds were soon busy with a second hatching of young, in another nest they had hurriedly repaired —and they learned to fly as their wing feathers grew out. In all other ways they continued to live as they had begun—happy, carefree, nosey busybodies—for a while. What eventually happened we deplored, but had to take, as the mockers themselves did, as something that was, is, and shall be as long as mockingbirds and humans last.

Pete Number One stuck his bill against the bait in a set rat trap one morning and was neatly guillotined. Three days later I found Ruthie Number One lying stiff on her back in the tomato bed, her claws cramped against her breast. We could not guess what had killed her.

Now we had only one Ruthie and one Pete. They stayed

with us two weeks longer. Then came a pair of really determined invaders and made dreadful war on Ruthie and Pete and their parents and the four little ones in the nest who were only old enough to cry "Eat, eat!" in weak voices.

Ruthie and Pete were chased away from home in the first day's struggle. The parents stuck it out a couple of days longer, though ragged and weak from strife and starvation. But they had to give up, and one morning the newcomers—the male bird with a lame, dragging wing—had taken over the place. The nestlings were left to death or the Conways. In the end both alternatives were the same thing.

We wanted no family responsibilities, but we could not stand the constant cheeping of the little birds nor watch their feeble and terrible struggles to get out of the nest. I could have given them an easy death, though Ainslie would not hear of it. He climbed the tree and gently lifted the nestlings into a tin can I had lined with torn-up paper.

It turned out that we were very bad foster-parents in spite of trying our best to be good ones. We spent a good deal of time catching moths and caterpillars and cleaning out the improvised nest—most of this work was mine though I had not chosen it—but all the young birds were dead within a week. Something must have been wrong with our feeding methods, and we felt guilty and a bit sick.

The new couple, Lame Wing and his mate, looked over the old nests in our compound and turned up their bills at all of them. They investigated every nook and limb and crotch for a new building lot and eventually chose a limb of the *aromo* tree which shaded our dining-table. Here they heaped up sticks and thorns, letting a good half of their building materials fall on the table. Other refuse fell on it, too. Without Ainslie's knowledge I poked the nest down a few times, but the birds were not discouraged. My own patience gave out first.

Lame Wing was a most terrific fence patroller, and that alone entertained us enough to earn forgiveness for almost anything else he might do.   Just after sundown he ran like a racing madman, his broken wing dragging up a trail of dust, to get in one more lap before bedtime. Ainslie is literally daffy about mockingbirds, but his affection for Lame Wing exceeded even the limits of daffiness.

One hot morning I had just washed the table-top for the third time when the need for washing it again appeared.   I was feeling low and irritable—very low and irritable. Lame Wing came down from the *aromo* for another twig, and, as was his custom, stopped a moment on the corral wall before going out on his searching trip. I picked up a handy stick, and with a sharp blow I caught Lame Wing on the back of the neck. He fell on his back, his legs still moving as if wanting to run.

I contemplated the bird's twitching legs and my own act with grim surprise. I had not really meant to kill Lame Wing. I felt so much like a murderer that when Ainslie came home I told him a sad story. "I aimed at a caterpillar crawling on the fence, and Lame Wing happened to get in the way," I said, thinking I was saving Ainslie's feelings as well as covering up my own guilt. Later I realised that saying nothing would have served both purposes better. Ainslie would have concluded that Lame Wing, in his birdlike way, had changed his mind about nest building or had been chased away by another mocking-bird.

Lame Wing's mate stayed with us a few days longer, searching and calling. She peered into the woodpile, the firebox, and under the beds, saying "Pete, Pete!" and, for a change, "Ruthie!" or "Ruthie, dear!" In the evening she patrolled the fence, but not as if her heart were in it. She moved in short spurts, stopping to look in crannies and call "Pete!" Eventually she gave up and went away.

The next morning another pair of mocking-birds were examining our living quarters.

XIII. HALLUCILIGHTS

In considering the hazards of living on a desert island or doing anything else which is unusual, almost anyone will think of the physical dangers first: What if you should die of starvation? What if wild and terrible animals should devour you? What if you should break your back or get galloping psittacosis? Not many think of asking: What if you should go crazy? What would you do if you found yourself sinking into depressions, fears, hallucinations, and heeby-jeebies?

What, indeed? When you go to a desert island voluntarily, as we did, you naturally provide yourself with food and clothes to last as long as you think you will need them; you do not choose a waterless island—though we almost did; nor do you pick out a place that is inhabited by man-eating beasts, or, if you do, you furnish yourself with weapons and other protection against them. But in respect to mental and emotional hazards you just take your head in your hands.

Isolation, which in many ways can amount to the same thing as no danger whatever, can be a danger in itself. The saving element here is that isolation is not unfamiliar to any of us. Most people live on desert islands. A desert island is essentially a limited, isolated place. What is the life-sphere of the average person but a limited, isolated place? He has his social contacts, but, even in his home town, there are doors where he dare not knock and say simply: "I came to have tea with you." The door-owner would think him a hopeless, blundering boor or a maniac and lock the door in his face.

He can go to other places, but not always when and where he pleases. He goes only when and where his income, work, and family responsibilities permit—with many people this means never and no place. And when he does travel, what kind of contacts does he make? Does he call on the mayor's wife or the rich big shot? No, he sees the same kind of people he would have seen at home, he eats in the same type of restaurants, stays at the same class of hotels. He really "gets away" very seldom. Even tourists in foreign countries generally flock to the kind of places they are used to and seek out their own kind of people. The ordinary person cannot so much as write a letter to "just anybody" and expect to get an answer.

The few visitors who came to our island looked at the physical aspects of it and concluded that we led a terribly lonely existence, forgetting that their own kind of isolation did not seem to them terrible because they were used to it. Ours did, because it was different. We admit that we felt the shadow of loneliness fairly often, but both of us have felt lonelier in New York than we ever felt on our desert island. It is a commonplace experience that there is no loneliness like that of a great crowd of perfect strangers, each bent on his own business.

At first, and always from time to time, we liked the loneliness. Two months in a crowded Guayaquil hotel, plus eight days on the overcrowded, overloaded, over-age *Calderón* would have made the most gregarious social butterfly love loneliness for at least a week. Of course we had each other and the animals and there was outside company, too, mostly tuna-fishermen, though we had to take them as they came.

If we had few outside contacts, they were the richer for being rare. What, on Manhattan Island, is one more person? On Santiago Island if the population had suddenly jumped to three—heavens, the excitement and commotion! A third person appearing unexpectedly at Conways' Landing was about as historic, relatively, as William the Norman arriving at Hastings.

With us loneliness was only a little thing. But there were a lot of other little things—monotony could have been the name for all of them, though they masqueraded as weariness, irritability, moodiness, boredom, and nostalgia. There was danger in these, too, familiar as they are to all of us, and we had to find counter-irritants for them or they swelled and festered. On our "Isle of Escape" we had to search for escape!

I was alone in El Corral for at least five hours every day, while Ainslie was at the spring or hunting and fishing. These divergent interests and locales were a good thing—we got some time away from each other. Our natures are compatible enough, but long months spent together, hour after hour, might have proved disastrous.

Even so, there were mornings when my nerves nag-nag-nagged to get out of camp and would not be appeased by a stroll to the beach to watch the pelicans and seals for the five-hundredth time or to Pirate Point to see if Isabela looked as beautiful and desolate as she had looked yesterday and every day for the last six months. On some of these nag-nag days I walked to the spring to wash sheets or just to see what was going on. But if I was in a nag-nag mood, Ainslie was likely to be in a pick-pick mood—his nerves, he said, often felt as if someone were picking out the ends with tweezers and leaving them hanging outside his skin. Trouble could pop up as easily as the cork from a bottle of fermenting beer.

I might throw my soapy wash-water too close to the water-hole or leave the drinking cup on the same ledge where Ainslie kept it, but two inches farther to the right. He might fire a pile of brush to windward of the place where I had hung my sheets or walk with his toes pointed too far out. On nag-nag and pick-pick days no troubles were little troubles.

Resolutions made during pleasant moods to keep the cork from popping had little effect. Given pressure enough, it popped anyway. Perhaps it was better so. Had the cork held tight, the bottle could have burst. We wondered sometimes how we would look, locked in a death grip and rolling over and over on our *patio* floor like a pair of fighting mocking-birds. Even in our worst nerve-twitching moods we could get a snicker out of that picture—and the snicker was good medicine.

Being no better—though, we hope, not much worse than other people—we sometimes took our irritation out on the animals. We spoke unkindly to our lonely dog, though, for-tunately for her, she did not know the difference between curses and baby-talk, and more than once I killed birds because I was feeling low; always I met retribution, however, in the form of feeling lower still.

One day a hawk tried so persistently to carry away a piece of meat I wanted for our own dinner that my lower impulses surprised me with a *coup d'état*. Of its own volition my hand reached for a club, though that hand was partly to blame for the bird's behaviour—it had been feeding him on meat for many days. I hit him on the head and he passed out. In a moment he recovered and tried to fly away. I hit him again. This time he looked at me with such wild, helpless reproach that I was sorry. Then I was infuriated that he should take so much killing and I smashed his head. His eyes were now filmed and horribly sad, and I was willing to let him live but it was too late. I had to end his suffering by beating him until he ceased to twitch.

Could this have been adventure, perhaps? Had the hawk been a moose and had I been armed with a high-powered rifle, most people would answer "Yes, indeed!" Yet where was the difference? Like the moose-hunter I had killed a creature whose only error was that he wanted to live. Perhaps the difference was that the moose-hunter would have felt elated and heroic and I felt like a criminal and a heel. Fortunately for our self-respect we had pleasanter tension-releasers in addition to cursing and killing.

Books, which the more intellectual dreamer about desert islands always considers the most effective first-aid in mental troubles, were high on our list too. Not the Ten Best, by any means—just any old printed matter. From the States we had brought a couple of dictionaries, a few Spanish classics, and several good text-books on biology. In Guayaquil we had picked up some unselected volumes that had evidently been brought there by *yanqui* soldiers or sailors—James Thurber, Rex Stout, and H. Allen Smith were among them. These few lasted us a long time. From time to time we got old magazines from tuna fishermen—*Lifes* and *Posts* mostly, though a good many of the volumes they loaded us with were "funny books" which we used only for starting fires. We were not that hard-up for entertainment.

These reminders of "home" helped some of our troubles, aggravated others. The fantastic fiction took us away from our surroundings, the articles kept us fairly well posted on what was going on in the world, and the colourful illustrations and the pretty, mechanical format were refreshing after so much of the "natural" and the home-made. But now and then they made us homesick. I would find myself dreaming of clicking my high heels along a sidewalk or picking up gadgets in dime stores and other fascinating emporiums—gadgets which would have lightened our labours and given cheer to our household.

On one occasion I was really "sent" by Elsie, the Borden cow. It was a hot day and I had spent all morning cleaning Ecuadorian earth and pebbles out of ten pounds of green coffee and roasting it in a large, hand-hammered vessel, known as a *baila*, over an open fire. Stretching out on my bed in the afternoon for an hour of relaxation, I reached for a *Post* and opened it, first thing, to Borden's intriguing advertisement—in that issue it was devoted to the virtues of instant coffee! I spent a half-hour reading the ad over and over, though I cannot say that I was helped by so doing. Civilisation of the Borden brand seemed very good to me then and getting any of it that day was as remote as the moons of Saturn.

Not even the most sentimental could have objected to some of the pastimes that answered with us for "escape-adventure." Sometimes, when I was alone in camp and the place seemed as far off and quiet as a grave on a dead planet, I would close my eyes and listen. I was so accustomed to the day's voices that at first I could pick out nothing except a pulse-beat in my own ears. Then, far away, a hawk screamed—a black hawk it must have been, for his "Quee-ank, quee-ank" was a little sharper than the grey hawk's call. Presently I became aware of the rhythmic rumour of the ocean, which had been there all the time. Now a finch said "Chink-chink, chink-chink-chink" and repeated it. The rooster squawked in alarm—he must have seen a hawk. Soon quiet again and my own heartbeat, then once more the hawk, the finch, two other finches. A mocking-bird said sharply, "Ruthie!" On the ocean side a seal coughed and from the same direction came the "plunk, plunk, plunk" of boobies diving for herring. A slapping noise in the water—that would be the seal again. Now a dry, scrabbling sound on the bedroom mat, where a lizard was running across it, and a soft, soft breath in the *aromo* leaves. By this time my ears were so keen that I could hear bumble-bees in the pumpkin blossoms and the dog barking at the spring a mile away. When I opened my eyes I felt as if I had been somewhere far away for many hours.

Each evening after dinner we always took a *paseo* to Pirate Point, where there was always a cool breeze and few mosquitoes, or to a little hill near El Corral which we called Hallucilight Hill. From these points we could see all there was to see—belated goats trailing off toward Sugar Loaf and bedding grounds, donkeys still grazing, rain or mist on the mountains, the sunset sky, the ocean, and Isabela. As darkness came we played a game, which could have been childish, but what else was there to play? The object of the game was to see which of us could spot a light first —either a real one or a "hallucilight," which, in our language, meant an optical illusion. If we stared at the horizon long enough, usually we could see a light there, though it was really only a trick of our optic apparatus.

"Light ho!" said Ainslie. "Near Albemarle Point."

I looked toward the northern tip of Isabela, but saw no light. "Must be a hallucilight. I don't see it."

Ainslie kept looking at the same spot. "Yes, light ho! About one-fifth of the skyline distance toward Albany. Must be the tuna-ship I saw this morning from the spring."

With my eyes I measured off the distance, and, sure enough, I too saw a gleam of light, faint but steady. "Light, all right, but pretty far. I wonder if that ship will come into the bay tomorrow."

Presently the light was lost beyond the horizon—the ship was not coming to Santiago. We kept watching the horizon until hallucilights danced all along the length of it. Time then to return to El Corral.

Since we went to bed at eight, sometimes earlier, and got up around six, and neither of us can sleep more than seven or eight hours of the twenty-four, we got into the habit of sleeping soundly for the first three or four hours, then staying awake for a long time before we finished our sleeping. This wakeful spell should have been a problem, but it was not. Our nights were often more adventurous than the days.

On a single night in March all this happened:

When I awoke the moonlight was bright and the air was perfectly still. The sweet fragrance of *aromo* blossoms came to my nostrils and I lay still, breathing it in. Soon it was mixed with *palo santo*—then all I could smell was *palo santo*.

Without realising it for a while, I found myself listening to a small sound like that of water dripping into an empty tin cup. Some compulsion made me count the beats, which came in groups between intervals of silence. Twenty beats so fast that I could scarcely keep up with my counting, then a gradual slowing down to a stop. The tinny beats went on, scarcely audible, while I tried to figure out what made them. Not rain, not pans or dishes rattling—I eliminated everything.

What's a little noise? you ask. Nothing, certainly, to an average city dweller. To us, on Santiago, every sound not immediately explicable, made us prick up our ears and hold our breaths. Strange places have that effect, and in our situation we could not afford to ignore anything mysterious.

Another sound so low that it generally did not register at all came through in the stillness—the swishing echo of the surf in the *muyuyu* leaves. After each crash of the surf came the soft answer from the leaves, as if they were saying "Hush!" to the ocean. That tiny, metallic beating I was also hearing—could that too have been caused by the surf? Could the surf, beating a hundred yards away, have made a tin cup knock against another? That would be an explanation, though who knows if the right one? It was no use asking Ainslie's opinion—he could not have heard it.

Ainslie stirred and made a low mooing sound in his sleep. At first I was startled. It sounded like a strange voice begging entrance at the gate.

"In some ways I don't like moonlight," I told myself. "Too disturbing. Ainslie loves it, yet he is sleeping through this like a farmer."

I got up, put on an old shirt that was at the foot of the bed handy for that purpose, walked through the *patio* where the *aromo* fragrance was strong, pulled aside the table that served to block the entrance at night, and strolled toward the beach. The dog came up behind me and licked my legs. I jumped, and shooed her away in a sharp whisper.

The night was fresh after the heat of the day. A full moon was floating in the clear sky. Orion leaned to westward and to the north the Dipper was about to fill itself out of the ocean. And like one of Ainslie's wind-blown datum points, the Southern Cross was lopped over on its side.

"The surf sounds like a chugging motor against the lava," I thought. (Sometimes the surf actually fooled us into thinking that a motor-boat was in the bay—perhaps wishful thinking.) "And my being out here in the middle of the night, with only the surf and the seals for company, should feel strange and unreal, yet it doesn't. I seem to be doing something very usual and natural." Perhaps I was trying to convince myself.

Pebbly white clouds were forming in the east, and a white veil of mist covered Sugar Loaf. "Looks like a fat negro girl on her wedding day," I said aloud.

"No," said Ainslie's voice behind me. "It looks like a fat chocolate pudding with whipped cream."

"So you are awake. The last I heard from you, you were mooing in your sleep like a sick cow."

"Could have been very easily. I was dreaming of cow-hunting on Floreana Island. I got pretty tired of beef there sometimes, but I could use a good steak right now."

"What I would like from Floreana at this moment is about five gallons of orange juice. Whenever I think of something to eat these days or nights, the first thing that pops into my head is a large, super-orangey orange. A fresh pineapple follows."

"First, give me ham every time."

"With all the meat we have here, you still dream of more meat."

"I seem to be a carnivore."

L

We watched a seal swimming in the moonlight and surveyed the ocean for a chance "Light ho" before returning to our beds.

Ainslie lighted his pipe of Ecuadorian "Fuerte" and smoked it under the mosquito net. I tried to smell the *aromos* and hear the tinkling noise, but nothing happened. Ainslie's tobacco was too strong, and crickets had awakened near-by.

"Do you hear the crickets?" I asked.

"I haven't heard a cricket since nineteen-eighteen. Too high-pitched."

"There's one under your bed. He makes a good loud noise."

"All I hear is the surf—and, ah, right now, the bray of a jug-headed son of a jackass. Must be that old white one back to be shot again. I have killed him seven times already."

"He has nine lives, probably. You'll have to kill him twice more."

"How I hate this killing, killing, killing! Yet if I don't shoot those bastards they mess up the water-hole and make the nights hideous. And most especially I hate to kill the same donkey, or his ghost, for the eighth time. Those old white donkeys are so much alike that I could swear they are all the same one."

The dog went up on the hill above El Corral, and a great to-do of barking and braying broke out.

"Here I go," groaned Ainslie as he reached for the loaded rifle. In his full coat of tan he climbed the hill in the moonlight.

"Hoopa!" I heard Ainslie shout. "Get going, you long-eared, jug-headed, hairy-legged——" That's as far as I got hearing Ainslie. A loud bray cut off his voice.

"Hoopa!" I heard again, a little farther away, and the clatter of hoofs.

Ainslie came back. "Didn't want to shoot any of them so close to camp," he said.

In less than five minutes the donkeys were braying on Hallucilight Hill, nearer this time. Ainslie put on a shirt before he went out again, which seemed to mean business. In a few moments there was a shot, then another. Again hoofbeats, braying, and the dog barking in the distance.

"I scared them, but I don't think any of them are dead," Ainslie said as he hung up the rifle. "Now all we need is the Raucous Bird."

"Bang!" said the tin roof.

"Speak of the devil!" said Ainslie, startled.

It was now my turn to get up. I pounded on the roof with a stick until the heron—it was he all right—flew on the corral fence, where he sat turning his head as if looking for something. I threw a pebble and it flew an inch from his bill. He pulled up his head a little and went on sitting. My next pebble hit him —I had had practice. He only squawked his annoyance. Another heron squawked on the beach, and our visitor went to investigate.

I had two sources of trouble that shaded from the hallucilight category toward the real.

One of these began with itching and partial deafness in my right ear. At first I did nothing about it, thinking that it was one of those things that pass as mysteriously as they come. But when the itching got too troublesome, I began to imagine an insect had crawled into the ear canal. I poked into it with a bobby pin—I knew all about not putting anything smaller than your elbow in your ear, thank you—and brought out a wad of wax and cotton. "Oh, yes," I thought, "that cotton I had been in the habit of stuffing in my ears in Guayaquil to keep out the night noises was at the root of the trouble." I kept digging until I could bring out nothing more. The next day the ear felt worse and ached a little.

I tried washing out the ear canal by pouring in salt water with a teaspoon. Still no improvement. Then I tried salad oil —this with the idea of dissolving the hardened wax. Now the ear felt better, but a couple of days later it was worse again. I decided that my treatment had something wrong with it and left the ear alone. It felt no better and no worse, and the condition stayed with me throughout out stay on the island. It was cured eventually though not by home medication.

The other trouble had always been in the back of our minds, I think, though we had not spoken of it. But one day when I was alone on Pirate Flat and Ainslie was somewhere miles away exploring the farther side of Sugar Loaf for another possible spring, it came to me with a jolt. I looked across at Isabela and mentally reviewed the life behind those blue desert craters—the settlements at Santo Tomas and Villamil and finally the convict camp. The convicts were said to be incorrigible and desperate and constantly making efforts to escape. "What if some of them did escape," I asked myself, "and managed to get a boat? They would head for Santiago first, since that was closest to Isabela and, moreover, inhabited by only two *gringos* and no soldiers.

How much respect would such visitors have for me, alone on the beach?"

Once started, I elaborated the picture. Even if the convicts did not manage to flee to Santiago, other horrors could happen. Strange, piratical fishermen sometimes made their headquarters on the isolated Galápagos beaches. Or suppose something should happen to Ainslie. He could fall seriously ill, or be crippled, or even die—I imagined him taking terrible chances on his hunting and fishing trips. Perhaps at that very moment he was lying somewhere at the foot of Sugar Loaf, broken and bleeding. If I should one day find myself the only living human on Santiago, what would I do? I realised with a sick pang that I did not even know how to load the rifle, much less aim and fire it. What a stupid desert islander I was!

That afternoon I surprised Ainslie by insisting that he show me how to handle the rifle. He thought the business rather unnecessary, for, he said, he was hardly ever out of sight of the bay, wherever he wandered, and could see any approaching craft long before it was close enough to land. I wanted to tell him that I was also thinking of being left entirely alone on the island, but thought better of it. Once the idea was in his head, he might have worried too much about it. Anyway, now that I knew how to use the gun, I was prepared to do what little I could in the emergencies I imagined.

Toward the end of the hot season one culminating straw was added to Ainslie's private load of irritation—he was entirely out of tobacco, and he had been a heavy smoker for nearly forty years.

During the winter, when tuna fishermen came ashore occasionally, he had kept himself supplied with cigarettes by helping the bait hunters spot schools of herring or by just talking enthusiastically about the bait he had seen a week ago. But those smokes were now only tantalising memories.

I had religiously saved all the butts I could be blamed for making—not more than three or four a day. Like any other typical *norteamericano,* Ainslie had thrown his away—and I had picked up those too whenever I found them, as I had salvaged all tobacco refuse abandoned by visitors.

On the first tobaccoless days Ainslie refused to smoke the butts, saying that since I had gone to the trouble of collecting them I should also have the pleasure of smoking them. But the time came when he raided my butt cache—with my encouragment, to be sure, for I was not really tobacco hungry. And one night I awakened around two o'clock to find him squatted beside his bed, digging in the loose earth between two slabs of sand-stone. The craving for tobacco had become so overwhelming that he could not sleep, and he had remembered that he had often ground out cigarettes in just that spot. He found a half-dozen stingy butts, which he rolled up in pieces of toilet paper and smoked then and there. Later on came days when he made special trips over trails and parts of the flat where he might have discarded butts recently or even months ago.

Butt-hunting was one of our recreations until, search as we might, we found no more. That was the time we began remembering the butt-lined streets of Oakland and other United States cities and developed a very low opinion of people who throw away cigarettes only half-smoked. They seemed to be to blame for our lack of tobacco on Santiago Island.

We had substitutes, as all Galápagans have for almost anything, but everything Ainslie tried was definitely not the right thing, though some things were more nearly right than others. He experimented with *muyuyu* leaves, tomato leaves, and *chala* leaves. We had heard of another acceptable substitute, burro dung, but not even Ainslie was far gone enough to sample it. He voted to stay with the *chala*. In the present state of the island *chala* leaves were relatively difficult to find. Every few days he would take off across the flats in search of a tree he remembered having seen on his hunting trips and return a couple of hours later with the entire top of the small tree on his shoulder. He let the leaves dry on the limbs and picked a pipeful when he wanted it. A little toasting over the coals made the smoke more savoury.

Even with substitutes in plenty, Ainslie had bad days. His head ached, his eyes smarted, and his nerve ends seemed to be hanging outside his skin, curling and writhing, he said. His irritability made the daily tasks burdensome at times, and he treated me to bits of Irish eloquence by way of relief. One day he came in from a goat hunt that had been exceptionally strenuous and looked at the depleted woodpile. There was plenty of the sort of wood I gathered—small, dead sticks that burned up fast —but none of the axe-and-machete variety necessary for cooking and curing the goat meat the next day. "Everything waits on me to do it," he complained. "I don't feel like doing anything at all—I'm all in. Yet I must hurry up to chop wood, then I must hurry up to skin that goat, then I must hurry up to take my bath before it gets dark, and all I feel like doing is to hurry up and die!"

L*

All that hurrying done, Ainslie hurried up to eat three great helpings of *frijoles refritos* and *roquette* leaves, topped them with two platefuls of rice swimming in chocolate sauce, and smoked a few pipefuls of *chala*. He decided to stay alive until morning.

Keeping ourselves in reasonable grooming was with us a pillar of morale. Like the fabulous Englishman, we bathed and dressed for dinner. Not in formal clothes, to be sure, but at least in something clean and whole. We cut each other's hair every third Sunday and Ainslie shaved every afternoon.

To me it seemed that Santiago life made Ainslie better-looking, me more gruesome. Except where his shorts covered it, Ainslie's body was a bronze statue and to clothe it was to put an overcoat on Apollo. No doubt my skin, where it was exposed, was almost as dark as Ainslie's. Under my shorts and halter I had glaring white bands—interesting enough design, I guess, like that fancied by some of the goats on the island. My face was leathery, my hands worse than any dishpan hands I have ever seen, and my hair was straight, wind-snarled, and faded. How I looked to a chance visitor I dared not think, though I had some comfort in the thought that my appearance was perfectly harmonious with my surroundings.

I could have avoided some of the annoyance of washing clothes in not quite enough water if we had become nudists. Nudism would have been sufferable except when the mosquitoes were biting or when it was cold. But we did not want to. Nudism for practical or compulsory reasons is one thing, but nudism on principle is something else. In the minds of most people nudism skirts the fringe of lunacy, and we were too close to that fringe already, being desert islanders, to care to push ourselves farther toward it. With us, hanging on to our pants was equivalent to hanging on to our sanity.

There were times when our dog was also a little daft. She was really worse off than we—there was only one of her species on the island. She was affectionate and we were never as responsive toward her as she would have liked. Not even interested enough to give her a name. She went wild with joy whenever there were visitors—once she tried to swim out to an anchored tuna ship. And each time after the callers had gone she spent hours sitting on the shore, her nose pointed seaward, and howling.

No doubt there was a glimmer of hallucilights in many of our daily activities and attitudes, though we did not always suspect it. What was the motive behind my oddment collection and Ainslie's concern about birds and purple and magenta fishlets? The Road of the Quechua Ladies was, in my opinion, all hallucilight, though Ainslie could not see it that way. I argued, womanlike, that not seeing it that way was in itself hallucilight.

And could it have been that our entire desert island adventure was the most illusory of our hallucilights? Not that we shall ever admit it consciously. "Light ho!" we say and are stuck with it.

XIV. HALLUCIHORRORS

THERE still remained a problem that was not lightened by clean clothes, solved by expertness with the rifle, nor wholly forgotten in comedy. This, for want of a better name, I called the Hallucihorrors. It had its roots in the residue of fear that lurks in our consciousness from the moment of our first squawk to the last agony. It is the mother of superstition, of devils, and of gods.

Have you ever been startled by a strange shape in the dark, heard thunder in a January blizzard, or seen the sky turn blood-red with the hissing lights of the Aurora Borealis? If you have, you know what I mean. You are fascinated and, though you will not confess it, deeply afraid. Something seems to be against nature.

There are many things in the Galâpagos, and especially on Santiago, that are against nature as we were used to it. Of course we knew with our higher brain that those things are quite as they should be in the Enchanted Islands; but the dark, slow-moving lower brain was not convinced of it. It felt that there was something wrong, and something wrong with such fundamentally reliable things as the sun, stars, and earth seemed to it vaguely awful. It refused to believe that darkness could naturally come so soon after sunset, that Orion could possibly look so very magnificent as he strode across the zenith at midnight, or that there could even be such a constellation as the Southern Cross. The island itself, with its limbo-like tufa flats, bristling lava flows, dead craters, strange vegetation and stranger animals, was *unnatural* too in the muddled judgment of that portion of our minds which gropes and feels rather than sees and thinks.

Add to this the quite unnatural element that we were only two—and, often enough, simply one—among so much that was odd and paradoxical and monstrous. Everybody knows that when we are alone we feel dread or fear of things which leave us quite unmoved when we are in a crowd. We were alone so far away—far away both in distance and in time. Not only travelling time—that was relatively a trifle, though we waited six months for our first batch of mail—but in geologic time. If the imported animals were subtracted, our island was still in the mesozoic era —elsewhere in the world that was finished at least fifty million years ago. And even the animals of a later age, the donkeys and goats, took us back to the very earliest, dimly-lit historical times. They reminded us of characters like Abraham and Isaac. If on our walks we had come upon a herd of satyrs or the smoking remnants of bloody sacrifice on crude lava altars we would scarcely have been astonished. Things like that seemed quite in keeping with certain moods of our landscape.

These reminders of Abraham and the Greeks were not really horrid at all—I found them, on the contrary, stimulating and amusing. Given time and a long enough stay on the island I could have hatched a whole mythology of my own and had fun doing it. But the images of Pan and other spirits began to build up a background on which more horrific shapes could grow.

First among my hallucihorrors was the lava, and even reason sided with unreason in contemplating it. Though it lay perfectly motionless and peaceful, its very appearance was suggestive of menace. Black it was—we all fear black more than colours —and ugly and barren. It was primeval chaos, formless and inimical to life. Though I scarcely thought of it consciously, I must have been darkly aware of its history. Not many years ago it had been a fiery, hissing, smoking inferno, and it could become that again if the old fumaroles awakened. On hot, hazy days I could believe that the heat waves were volcanic smoke and actually smelled something sulphuric and metallic. Added to this imagined activity was the startling fact that fishermen once reported seeing smoke on the south side of the island. Oddly, I would have welcomed something of the sort on our side too —in reasonable measure, that is. The tension of suppressed expectation would have been relieved. Two months after we left Santiago one of the sleeping craters of Isabela did erupt, and we deplored that it had not happened while we were still in our ringside seat on Pirate Point to watch it. This proved to me that it was not always the real danger implied by new lava that obsessed me. The trouble was that my lower mind saw the lava as a beast, a monster, an evil god.

Another phase of the fundamental horror caught me nearly every time when I went out to gather wood. With me wood-gathering is generally pleasant business—I am getting my fuel "for nothing" and I have a good walk in the open air. During my first stay in the Galápagos I had never encountered unpleasant complications on such excursions, except once when I got lost in the wild-bull pastures of Floreana. On the Santiago flats I could not possibly get lost and no wild animals threatened me, yet I hated my wood-gathering chore until the thought of it made me sick.

Ainslie could not understand my aversion to a task I had previously enjoyed, and I could not explain it to him clearly enough. It was not that he could not understand extraordinary moods—he has enough of his own—but that he could not see how a feeling so far-fetched was conjured up by an activity so commonplace. It took me a long time to understand it myself, partly because I also had an aversion to analysing it.

"Dead sticks among dead bones on a dead land," I said to myself as I gathered my squaw wood on the flat and in the gullies, and it occurred to me finally that the word "dead" was the key to my feeling. I stopped to gaze around on the empty flat and the empty sea. Everywhere nothing living. Only the wind blowing, the seas breaking—all alien, all self-contained, all indifferent. And dead though my surroundings seemed, there was nevertheless something alive in the emptiness and deadness. Something alive that was totally unmindful of me yet, paradoxically, threatening. The indifference itself was the menace. Anything could happen to me, and the island and the sea would remain imperturbed as if nothing had happened. I was not needed, not wanted, not noticed.

I hurried with my load of wood toward the safety—so it seemed—of the corral walls. When I turned my back to the flat I was tempted to look around. I had turned my back on a danger that was surely stalking me. I looked behind me. Nothing there, of course, nothing I could see. Yet, if I did not hold myself steady with a conscious effort, I would hasten my steps, even run until I was back in the home gully, and beside my familiar fireplace.

The ocean too was a paradox and my reaction to it paradoxical. Fundamentally I am a lover of the sea and it fascinates me. The sea is always the same and always changing, always predictable and always surprising. On Santiago I felt it as a friend and an enemy. All the "good" that we sometimes craved —change, companionship, eventual "rescue"—had to come from the sea. It was always a barrier too—the Great Barrier that limited our horizon, hemmed in our island, kept us from travelling to other places. It was full of life, the original mother of it, yet it was also empty. It was even more indifferent to us than the desolate land and at the same time seemed ready to catch and overwhelm us.

Sometimes when I awoke to a dark night and heard the surf pounding on the cliffs, which were our very gates, I could feel its immensity and power, and, as if crawling along my nerves, our aloneness and the fragility of our island.

"What keeps the ocean out?" I could have asked like a stone-age savage, in my half-awakened state. Why does it not come in and wash right over us? The Galápagos stand high on their pedestals on the deep, deep ocean floor. How strong are those pedestals? Couldn't the breakers wash right through them some dark night? What if the island should slip loose from its moorings, slide a little with the current, then splash sidewise into the depths and sink and keep on sinking?

This illusion of danger was silly, of course, in the everyday view of things—a view supported by civilised comforts and the presence of many other people. It was as silly as the feeling of security we all have in our comfortable beds, behind glazed windows and locked doors, while other families sleep above and below us and in the apartment across the hall. What could other people have done against the cosmic dangers my paleolithic mind was contemplating? Yet, had we had a dozen noisy companions, the rumbling of the ocean would have passed unheeded. This dreadful panic which most of us feel when we find ourselves alone on the naked earth, face to face with the universe, is what makes people refuse to live on a desert island, much as they may dream of living in some illusory bit of paradise.

During the hot season when the winds came mostly from the north and west, which were our seaward quarters, we could smell the ocean. This may not seem odd to everyone; living on the seashore we should have smelt it. However, when the trade winds prevailed, they had to cross the island to reach us and were so loaded with land smells—dust, goats, *palos santos*—that the ocean smell was diluted or overwhelmed. On the days when we smelt the ocean we could also hear it most distinctly. The northerly winds pushed the rollers against the cliffs and lava heads, where they foamed and smoked and roared as if trying to tear them down. That, of course, was just what they were doing, though not fast enough to catch me in my corral. But the smell was even more suggestive—the ocean seemed to have reached our very nostrils.

There are no storms in the Galápagos seas. When storms far to the north sometimes drove a heavy swell into our seas, the fact that the source of the turmoil was elsewhere made the tom-tom beat of the surf oddly meaningful. An all-powerful, unknown enemy was far away, but coming nearer. To hear these tom-toms we had to be in a disturbed, dark-minded mood. At other times the surf sounded just like surf.

On the many days when there was no swell at all and the water at Conways' Landing was so relaxed that it scarcely slip-slapped against the sand, the mood of unreasoning dread went away. Though not always—the very silence became at times ominous. I could imagine the ocean sneaking up to catch me unawares. This really perverse fear could easily be cured: merely walk to the ocean and look at it. Sparkling sunlight and clear blue water to the horizon. Sparkles and pretty colours make a child or a savage reach out his hands and grasp—not even the most rudimentary minds are afraid of them. At such times I could stand on the clean sand and let the waves ripple over my feet or wade out knee-deep and actually think of swimming. I never did swim, however—it was enough for me to bathe in the tide pools. Ainslie swam occasionally, though he too preferred to do it close to shore. We really had a good excuse—neither of us is an expert swimmer and the bay was full of sharks.

In an old magazine I happened to read an article about tidal waves, and for weeks afterwards I was obsessed by them. Tidal waves have never been heard of in the Galápagos. "They can't happen here," my reason said, but my emotions were not convinced.

Every day I was on the beach rocks washing beans or meat and I always kept an eye on the incoming waves, even when the ocean was calm and the tide low and the water could not possibly rise high enough to wash my beans or me into Neptune's pocket. If a wave did splash a little higher than I had expected, I moved back fast but sneakingly, so that Ocean would not know I was scared.

By way of documentation, I have this entry in my diary for March 11th:

This morning there was an exceptionally low tide, and Ainslie and I went out on the reef below Pirate Point to see what the receding waters had uncovered. Ainslie took a bucket, for edible fish large enough for the frying pan were sometimes left trapped in the tide pools, or—perhaps just this once—we could find a lobster where we need not wade neck-deep for it.

While Ainslie knelt on the lava with his back to the ocean and beamed like a doting grandmother at tiny fish that crawled on their fins over the bottom of a pool, I remained strictly on my feet and looked around as casually as I could for shells to add to my collection, for, in spite of the presence of another person, a Tidal Wave was approaching.   The sea was as mild as milk, but that was just another trick.   I looked landward.   How long would it take me to reach the shore if the Wave suddenly whooshed over the rocks?   I would have to hop over a good four rods of broken lava, some of it still slippery with wet seaweed.   I was sure I could not make it in time.   I did not worry about Ainslie's safety—the Wave did not menace him.   How could it, for it was only in my mind?

"Don't be an ass!" I told myself.   "Or, rather, do be one.   A donkey has better sense than to worry about tidal waves."

No good.   The Tidal Wave kept on coming.

"Well, I know one way to get this obsession out of my mind.   I'll just get off these accursed rocks!"

That was what I did, which was a pity.   It was a beautiful day for that season, an excellent time to linger a while on a far-sought and exotic reef.   Ainslie scolded me for showing so little interest in creatures that some scientist friends of ours would have given anything to collect and study.

"I forgot my sun-glasses," I said.   "I'm going to get them."

When I returned, wearing the glasses, I busied myself diligently studying the crabs and limpets on the sand of the Landing—a place easy to escape from if the Tidal Wave came.

In justice to myself I can say that I have scrambled over plenty of rocks on other seashores, without feeling any dread—acute or vague—of tidal waves and other such rare carriers of catastrophe. In fact, I am considered rather intrepid—at least by really timid persons.   But on Santiago the strangeness and aloneness awoke a basic dread and some incident or bit of information could crystallise the feeling into an image.   Perhaps another reason for creating images of fear was that I had too few real fears or pre-occupations to drive out the hallucinations. When immediate and acute concerns are not present the vague, shadowy ones begin to take shape and grow. And how they do grow!

Occasionality reality took a swipe at us too. Once a tidal wave *did* catch me. So perhaps I was only "psychic" about my Waves and not going crazy after all.

One afternoon I went with Ainslie to his favourite fishing hole—a deep, narrow inlet between two arms of lava jutting out into the ocean. Ainslie sat on the edge of it to angle for *cabrillo*. He offered me a baited line, but I just could not fish in *that* hole and the more innocent-looking ones harboured no fish.

I wandered off to explore the shore for curious rock formations, seal bones, and whatever else I could find. I was careful not to go too far on the lava seaward, for the tide was on the way in.

A stretch of lava which was at least a hundred feet from the nearest breakers seemed smooth and solid, and, I judged, well above the level of high tide. I sat down on a cosy, chair like ridge to watch Ainslie land a three-foot shark.

There was a sudden whroomp of water behind me, which was landward, and I was streaming wet and swallowing sea water. I jumped up and realised that I was still on solid lava and could breathe air. Water flowed at my feet and I moved away but rapidly—no sneaking escape this time. Then I looked back to see where the great splash of water had come from. Another geyserlike column burst out of the lava, paused a moment in mid-air, and broke over the rocks. There was a hole in the lava just behind the ridge where I had sat. Evidently the incoming tide found an under-surface passage and pushed up through the hole.

I went to tell Ainslie that I was going back to camp to wash salt water out of my clothes. At that moment a good barrelful of ocean slapped Ainslie's face, and he too had reason to go back to camp. "Probably that was a gentle hint from old Neptune that two *cabrillos* are enough for two people," he said as he wound up his line.

On the way home I considered my distrust of both lava and ocean, two things we had in plenty. From the top of the flat we could see the great flow, and at the seaward edge, where the red rocks rose up like an enchanted castle, the tide rushing fiercely against the black monster.

"I can imagine myself building an altar on top of those red rocks," I said. "How exciting that would be! A great fire burning, a bloody, murdered goat smoking in the nostrils of the black demon, and the ocean roaring and spitting as if in jealous rage! Or do you think that is too far-fetched?"

"Too far-fetched!" Ainslie scoffed. "On the contrary, too damned close!"

XV. HAVE YOU SEEN BAIT? HAVE YOU
SEEN HITLER?

From the first day we had wondered who our first callers would be. Certain visitors we had reason to expect. The commander of the *Calderón* had assured us that his ship would return in two months, when she was expected to make the next official tour of the inhabited Galápagos ports; Hans Angermeyer had said that he and his brothers were interested in Santiago as a possible place of settlement and would take time in the winter to come on a tour of exploration in their sailboat; the American commander of the Baltra base had promised to send a scouting plane within three weeks of our arrival and, if possible, the tugboat later on, though not entirely for our benefit; the "boys" would enjoy a hunting expedition. None of these visits materialised and, in the end, it made no difference.

Yet, six weeks after we landed, we heard a human voice not our own. One morning, so early that we were not quite awake, the surf sounded, as it often did, just like a motor-boat. We listened for a while, trying to make up our minds. Was it the surf? Was it a motor-boat? "Surf," I said. "Motor," said Ainslie. So convinced was he that he pulled on shorts in a hurry and ran down to see what was up. As soon as I was presentable I followed.

A boat was there, skirting the shore, and in it were three men. Ainslie waved to them. The boat slowed a bit as it came opposite the landing, and the man standing at the prow cupped his hands to his mouth and shouted: "Have you seen any bait?"

"Lots of it," Ainslie shouted back.

"Where?"

"All over the bay! The boobies and shearwaters were fishing like mad last night!"

The boat buzzed around the bay a couple of times and then rounded the point out of sight. We clambered to the top of the flat to see. Standing off to the west was a smart, white tuna ship. The boat approached it, was pulled aboard, and the ship went away toward Isabela.

So that was the nature of the attention tuna fishermen gave

to a couple of desert islanders, who, for all they knew, were castaways and about to perish! Inhabitants on Santiago should have astonished them, for on the charts the island was marked uninhabited. Curiosity was what these fishermen had not. Or, rather, they had plenty of it, but they reserved it all for fish.

Had we been in acute need of communicating with outsiders we could have hung a white sheet on a pole at the beach, as a signal of distress. But—no distress, no signal. Though a fire is generally taken as a call for help on lonely sea-coasts, we knew it would not be heeded. Several times we had happened to have a large brush fire going when a tuna ship was in sight, but no one on the ship had showed the slightest interest in it as far as we could see. They were no doubt so single-minded in following their beautiful silver-skinned money fish that they were practically unconscious of the island. If they saw smoke they thought they were seeing mist or perhaps volcanic fumes. The chances were that they did not even notice it.

Three weeks after the bait-hunters had hailed us with their characteristic question, two tuna ships rode at anchor all night within hailing distance of the Landing. Their lights, gleaming red, green, and white on the black water and against the black bulk of Old Crater, gave us the feeling that we had suddenly been transported to a busy, metropolitan port. The fishermen slept quietly all night on one side of the little stretch of water and sandstone, the Conways on the other side. At dawn both ships pulled out.

By this time we had concluded that tuna fishermen were absolutely unsociable persons. They could, of course, have drawn the same conclusion about us, though we did not look on it from that angle.

The winter months are the heavy tuna fishing months in the Galápagos, and a few days later another streamlined white ship anchored close in. It was two hours before sundown, an unusually early hour for these fishermen to bed down for the night, but we were educated now and did not expect any landing parties.

A half-hour later ten men—count them, ten!—walked up to El Corral. At first sight they were pretty rough customers and very, very dark. Did I read in their eyes, which in several instances were blue, the same opinion of us? Most of these *hombres* were of Portuguese ancestry and wore black whiskers many weeks old. One was Japanese and two were Mexicans, who, on the other hand, were counterbalanced by a couple who looked like Swedes. Their ship, they said, had left San Diego,

California, ten weeks ago, and they had been dogged by bastardly fishing luck. (No tuna fisherman in his right mind ever boasts of good luck until at least a year after he has experienced it.)

"What's going on in the world lately?" Ainslie asked after he had answered why we had come to the island, what we were doing there, and how long we intended to stay.

"The usual, I guess," answered a tow-headed gent who was the engineer. "We haven't seen a paper for over two months and we never listen to radio news."

"Then you don't know any more than we do," Ainslie commented.

"If as much."

The Japanese, who had been eyeing our camping arrangements through dark-rimmed glasses, asked without preliminaries: "Mr. Conway, just what percentage of your diet would you say consists of fish?"

"So far, zero. I have not had much time for fishing yet."

The Japanese seemed to find the answer interesting. He looked like a studious chap; perhaps he was doing some research in comparative eating habits.

The visitors stayed an hour, though only three of them did any talking. Then they said good-bye for themselves and the others who had not come ashore and returned to their ship, which would leave before dawn.

We did our chores, cleaned up for the evening, and filled ourselves with warmed-over rice and goat stew. It was getting dark when we heard more visitors approaching.

This time the delegation consisted of seven—all those who had not been ashore before. Among them was an immense young man who carried on his shoulder a large packing-box. This he set down on the table and then introduced himself: "I am Joe, the cook."

Once his mouth was open, he seemed incapable of closing it. Words kept getting in the way. These were a few of them:

"Those guys came aboard and told me they had visited you and right away I asked, did you invite them to dinner? Of course they hadn't and that sure burned me up. I had one of the finest meals ready that I have ever cooked, and let me tell you that I have cooked some mighty fine ones. Those guys like good food all right—just try giving them what isn't good and you'll find out. Some of these tuna ship cooks sure can ruin food faster than a shark can ruin a bait net, but I am not one of those steak burners. I am a good cook. But do those guys ever act like the food was better than anybody else's? Not them. They gobble it up like a shark eating bait and leave the table without saying a word. Never a peep about how good the food was. Now I like my cooking to be appreciated—I'm like an artist that way. Those guys sure burn me up. Here tonight I have plenty of real food ready to serve to six extra guests, not only two—people who could really appreciate it, and what do they do? Forget to invite you. Sure burned me up. So what do I do? There's more than one way to bait a hook, I always say. I packed some of everything we had for dinner, and a few other things, in this box and brought it over. The other guys woke up then and gathered up some old magazines we had cluttering up the cabins and a few packs of cigarettes. They're all in the box there. Oh, where's the ice water? Good, I see you brought it, Tony. I filled this cider bottle, with cold fresh water, distilled water it is, made by our own engines and ice cold. You better have a swig of it right now before it gets warm. I bet you have not had a real cold drink for two months and can appreciate it. And sit down right now, and I'll dig out the steaks I brought. They are still warm—I put a few yards of wax paper around them."

While we listened and wondered what under heaven we could say to this young man to show that we really did appreciate his cooking, no matter how bad it turned out to be, our "host" pulled tomatoes, sweet peppers, green onions, lettuce, a loaf of bread, and the steaks out of the box. He glanced around and saw where I kept the dishes. He got out plates, cups, and stainless steel, which with us answered for silver. In a jiffy he arranged two plates of salad and dressed them with French dressing he had brought in a pop bottle. With loving care he laid the sirloins on the largest plates and flanked them with green onions. He filled the cups with ice water.

"Now!" he invited. "Food is always best eaten fresh."

We had to eat what he set out and do our best to rave about it. Our best was pretty good, I think, though we were already stuffed with rice and goat. When he saw us actually eating, the cook was silent, listening to our words of praise and beaming as we chewed. He stirred the fire to give us light to eat by.

When, eventually, our plates were cleaned up and we sat back with sighs—sighs of regret for having eaten anything all day long before this elegant windfall hit us—the cook rummaged in the box again. He brought out half a cherry pie and cut it in two pieces. He rummaged again and came up with a slab of cheese.

"I would have brought a whole pie, but half was all I had left," our benefactor said as he set the dessert in front of us.

'*Dios mío!*," I remonstrated inwardly. "You do have the knack of sending the right thing at the wrong time!"

Joe really was a good cook, fully as good as he said he was. Sometime, when and if we get that long-coveted fishing trip on a tuna ship, we pray that Joe is the cook. That is, if he is not yet steak chef at the Fairmont.

When the seven finally went back to the ship, Joe assured us that the next time he was around he would come ashore personally, to invite us to dinner—he would not trust those other guys. Burned him up.

As it happened, Joe the Good Cook did not come again. But other cooks came—comparatively lesser artists, but still good. They were accompanied by good captains—Manuel the Good Captain, Tony the Good Captain, Joe the Good Captain, and there were Manuel II and Joe II, also good captains. One captain was described by his crew as "crazy," but they meant "funny crazy" not "real crazy." He was a Good Joe, too.

When the fourth of our tuna-hunting visitors from San Diego anchored in James Bay, the captain himself, a Good Tony, came to invite us on board. Captain Tony had troubles, as the Good Cook had had steaks, and he wanted to share them with someone. He had been in the Galápagos almost as long as his food and oil rations permitted, and his freezing tanks were still two-thirds empty. Bad luck had followed him as a shark follows a school of smelt and had done about as much damage. Good Tony was worried that worrying about no tuna in the tanks was worrying him into a case of stomach ulcers and worrying so much about the symptoms of incipient ulcers that he was worried that he really was getting ulcers and that was what worried him. The reason that he had no tuna was that he had found no bait. And what really crowned his misfortunes was that he had seen any number of spots where the ocean was literally boiling with tuna. Oh, and he needed a good load of tuna—really needed it—for he had had bad luck on his previous trip, too, and was up to his neck in debt. Only a good school of smelt and herring in James Bay the next morning could save him.

Tuna fishermen are in the habit of throwing live bait into the sea where there are signs that tuna are present. The big fish, which travel in schools, rise to snap up the small fish and usually go so mad that they snap up anything, even a plain, unbaited hook. Then all the fishermen have to do is throw in their barbless hooks, attached with strong lines to bamboo poles, and as the fish are snagged toss them on deck with a skilful movement of the pole. There is no need to bait hooks or to remove fish with the hands. Sometimes, if the fish in the school are very large, two or more poles are fastened to one hook and several men work in unison. When the fish are really biting, action is hectic and the money fish pile up on deck hip-deep, for no one has time then to put them in the freezers. That is a job for later when the fish have ceased biting.

Some such picture was in Good Tony's mind—and only there as far as he was concerned, where it was doing him no good. Now here was a case. We really wanted to help, but what could we do? Had our wishes been fishes, the bay would have been one vast cauldron of bouillabaisse the next morning. Tuna fishermen had been so friendly with us, friendly beyond any call of duty, that we wanted to pay back their kindnesses to one of them at least. This captain was a good payee, because his need was sore and his cook, not content with the hot biscuits, the lobster salad, and the lemon pie he had fed us, had promised us a chocolate cake the next time he came around.

It is no joke that we prayed as earnestly as we are able that night: "Bait for Tony in the morning! Please, whoever hears and cares and *can*, bait for Tony in the morning!"

If only the prayers of the righteous avail, then our righteousness was permanently established the next day.

At the crack of dawn we were startled awake by the frantic barking of the dog. Between yaps we could hear the excited plunk, plunk, plunk of boobies diving near shore and the splashes and cries of pelicans and gulls. Mixed with these were the shouts of men and the sound of oars. Bait in the bay! That we had to see.

Herring and other small fish were gathered in an immense school so close to shore that we could see them from where we stood. There was a sort of boiling on the surface of the sea, and boobies, pelicans, and gulls swooped, and squawked and dived. Shearwaters in even greater numbers fluttered and dipped, just touching the water on the down-stroke but never diving. Each dip brought up a fish. Captain Tony and his boys were as busy as the birds. Incipient ulcers had taken a vacation.

Tony's crew had taken up their bait nets after a third and last fat haul, when another, larger tuna clipper, the acknowledged "queen" of the fleet, came unexpectedly around the point and straightway anchored a stone's throw from Tony's ship and had her nets down before the anchor chain had ceased rattling. The captain of the newcomer—he was Good Joe I—filled his bait tanks too. Birds were still fishing when he hauled in his nets, though hundreds of them had settled on the rocks to doze and digest.

Each of the ships sent us a box of magazines and cigarettes and a quart of chocolate ice cream. We had been so busy watching that we had not had time to cook. The ice cream filled us up neatly, though I did wish that chocolate could be less popular with our benefactors.

The "queen" was the first to make off at top speed for the right tuna spots—Good Joe knew them all. He must also have been psychic, or how else could he have known that our prayers of the night had been answered so extravagantly? Worry Bird Tony did not come back to our harbour and we heard that Bad Luck was still fishing with him. But Good Joe came several times, and we had a standing invitation to come aboard his ship whenever he was in the vicinity. He had bedded down some fifty tons of tuna with the bait our prayers had provided.

Tuna ships have elegant names, evidence that their owners think highly of them. One day the *Princess Pat*, the *Queen of the Pacific*, and the *Glory of the Seas* were anchored at one time in James Bay, and a fine-looking fishermen's harbour they made of that lava-bound stretch of blue water which still seemed to be sleeping far back in lost geologic ages.

Such a romantic view of James Bay was our own, strictly. To the fishermen it was only a good place to anchor or to get bait, and the island itself was nothing but a name or at best a sort of datum point. Some of the tuna fishermen had been coming to the Galápagos for years and had never been ashore on any of them.

In regard to visitors we actually expected the unexpected, but we were surprised when the yacht came. On a winter afternoon Ainslie had just gone up the canyon, bent on the usual goat hunt, when I happened to see a tall spar moving behind the bushes that screened us from the bay. Without stopping to investigate, I ran after Ainslie to call him back. It was the day when I had been learning to load the rifle, and I was not in the mood to receive strangers alone. I did not quite trust my aim yet.

A dinghy had already been beached when we came panting down to the Landing. "How are you doing, Conway?" shouted a barefoot man walking toward us on the sand.

"Mac, of all people!" gasped Ainslie. "What brings you back to the Galápagos?"

It turned out that Mac was an old friend Ainslie had known while the two were employed building the Baltra base during the war. The owner of the tall-masted schooner, *Norseman*, was Tucker McClure, a big-name contractor in the Canal Zone. He had built Albrook Field, among other places, and been Ainslie's and Mac's employer at the base. Mr. McClure and another friend of ours, Captain Baverstock, a Canal pilot, were on board, as well as still another Canal pilot, Captain Small. On her present trip, the *Norseman* was the best-manned ship we have ever encountered. Any of the four men on her was capable of being captain, pilot, navigator, cook, crew, or what do you want? They were all yacht-enthusiasts and were or had been yacht owners.

That evening, instead of butchering a goat, we had dinner on the *Norseman*. Tucker McClure himself, a grey-haired one-time Colorado sheepherder, wearing jeans and a red handkerchief tied around his head pirate fashion, cooked and served the meal.

While on Santiago, Captain Baverstock and Captain Small wanted to celebrate their presence with a goat barbecue, Argentine style. Ainslie tried to talk the whole gang into a pig hunt or an exploring trip into the mountains, but only Captain Baverstock was interested. The others looked on the lava flow they would have to cross with deep distrust in their eyes. Baverstock had stars in his—he is a Galápagos enthusiast—but he had a badly sprained knee and distrusted that.

The next day Baverstock and Small killed and butchered a fairish doe, and the Conways provided the barbecue equipment and two immense piles of dead trees and brush we had cleared out of the canyon but not yet burned. Being something of a pyromaniac, I personally fired the brush piles, an hour apart, to ensure a steady supply of coals.

After anointing it with a sauce of oil, vinegar, and seasonings, the hunters staked out the entire carcass over the embers. In three hours the experts pronounced the goat ready to eat. It was well crisped and lightly smoked on the outside. A knife stuck into a round brought out a gush of red juice.

When one eats barbecue, Argentine style, each guest cuts his meat from wherever on the carcass he prefers. The visitors laughed at the thick chunks I hacked off. They liked theirs in very thin slices, well peppered and salted, as if hunting and roasting the goat had been better fun than the eating of it. McClure was frank in confessing distaste. "I herded so many sheep in my boyhood that now I can't stand anything that reminds me of them," he said. Only continued coaxing made him accept a tiny sliver, which he ate like a cat trying to keep grease out of his whiskers.

When she sailed away the following day, the *Norseman* took away a bunch of letters for us, the first we had mailed since leaving Guayaquil.

During our eight months on Santiago, only one visiting woman set foot on it. Mrs. Thornton came on the *Pearl Harbor,* a shark-fishing vessel whose home port was San Francisco. She was the wife of the captain and had come on the trip "for the fun of going places." She was paying for her fun by cooking for a crew of some dozen men in a hot little galley, and she said she did *not* like cooking! Three things about this adventurous lady were to me remarkable: her abundant red hair, done up in perfect curls—by contrast it made me feel like a witch; her excellent hot rolls, and the canned apricots she gave us for dessert. At that time I had been dreaming regularly of canned apricots—in my dreams I would open a can, reach for a spoon to cram the fruit into my mouth, and then the can would disappear.

The apricot deal turned out to be even better than a good dishful. The *Pearl Harbor* was short on sugar, of which we still had nearly three hundred pounds, and long on flour, our leading "all gone" commodity. At the captain's suggestion we exchanged fifty pounds of sugar for fifty pounds of flour. Since sugar was more expensive than flour, Mrs. Thornton added six cans of apricots and six of other fruit to the ship's end of the transaction. Everybody was happy.

On his own part Captain Thornton gave us a couple of surprises. Upon landing, his first words to Ainslie were: "Dr. Livingstone, I presume?" We had heard that one a good many times! Then he suddenly asked: "You haven't seen Hitler around, by any chance?"

"And just why Hitler?" Ainslie wanted to know.

"Well, there's a queer story going around the islands. They

say that a few weeks ago members of the Baltra garrison appeared unannounced at the Wittmer house on Floreana, with fixed bayonets, and proceeded to search the premises. The bayonet boys explained that a report had come to the base about Hitler hiding somewhere in the Galápagos, and the home of the German Wittmers seemed the most likely place."

We all laughed at the rumour, of course, and months later, when we questioned the officers of the base about it, they said that they had not even heard the story. But while we were on Santiago we kept thinking about the business, perhaps because we secretly wished to have Hitler with us. What better way for obscure desert islanders to become names in history?

While we did not credit the story, we admitted that Hitler's hiding in the Galápagos was not impossible—his death had not yet been proved—and why not on Santiago? The idea was not nearly so fantastic as it had appeared on the first look. An escape ship could have landed at James Bay, and who would have known it? Even we, with the little we had, could have continued to exist on the island—barring accidents, which have to be barred anywhere—for who knows how many years. Hitler with his resources would have found it much easier. We never went far enough into the mountains to prove to ourselves that Hitler was not there, and clever camouflaging, of which Hitler's companions would certainly have been capable, could have hidden all signs of habitation from any scouting planes which might fly over the island.

Another game was added to our hallucilight play. Whenever we missed anything or mislaid it, we blamed it on Hitler. And whenever a donkey brayed in the distance, we said: "There speaks Hitler."

Planes in our sky were indeed rare, though I suppose there is not a spot of earth left from where they are not to be seen occasionally. Some of the tuna-fishing companies sent scouting planes, but the pilots of these were interested in the ocean, not the land. A few times bombers from the base flew high over the island, as if Santiago were much too insignificant to look at closely. To the pilots of those planes, who had bombed Pacific islands until they were blue in the face, what was another island?

We had been on Santiago six months when one quiet afternoon a bomber came in flying low between Albany and Old Crater. There seemed to be no doubt that this plane was for us, but with what mission?

M

In a couple of minutes the bomber was buzzing El Corral. In a daze of excitement we ran up Hallucilight Hill and lighted a pile of trash, so that the smoke might indicate the direction of the wind in case the flyers intended to make a drop.

The plane was so large and its noise so island-shivering that I almost expected it to lay a dozen highly-explosive eggs. Instead, when it had lost enough altitude, the monster spit out a tiny parcel with some sort of rag fluttering from it. In the slip stream the package broke and the pieces were scattered among the weeds and brush of a near-by canyon.

Ainslie recovered a couple of fragments and waved them above his head to indicate to the flyers that their mission had been successful. The plane went away directly, and we spent a half-hour looking for the other pieces, which turned out to be letters and a khaki pants' leg that had served as a streamer. We found eleven letters and worried for ever after that we had not found them all.

Evidently our mail had been left at the base by an Ecuadorian ship.

That was the only time we received mail, but the delivery was so dramatic that the one time was more satisfying than a dozen less spectacular deliveries would have been. Perhaps it was not surprising that after the shock of receiving them we found the letters about as exciting as old advertising folders. Human emotions have their limits.

XVI. THE CASE OF THE MISSING GOAT

June had come and with it the best of the "pure Galápagos" weather. The Ecuadorian calls it summer, but in our opinion it has a closer correspondence to the temperate-zone winter.

Our flats were dry and brown, the mountains played hide-and-seek with the mists, and the south-east trades were as steady and punctual as time and tide. The ghostly *palos santos*, which seem to spend most of their existence in a sort of life-in-death, had lost their leaves. All creatures had ceased breeding. Our world was now at rest—self-contained, remote, quiet. The wind, the surf, and the bird voices came to us so blended with the all-pervasive serenity that they were only the attributes of silence. Living on our beach was like living in a melancholy dream that is forgotten as soon as the dreamer awakes. Death had been added to life, and the sum divided by two.

Life like that is good for a while, as starving is good for a while. Food tastes more than naturally excellent to a man who has not had enough to eat for months, and coming back to life is exciting after having been dead—or as dead as it is permitted us to be without crossing the borderline. Any savage experiences that kind of vegetative equilibrium during the months when life in nature is in abeyance, as it is in the temperate-zone winter or in the dry seasons of some tropical areas. The civilised man misses it, partly because his winter climate is so severe that it keeps him hopping to avoid freezing and, for the rest, because he has added duties, distractions, and unnatural comforts to his existence. Our "pure Galápagos" season, on the other hand, was mild enough to let us relax and so "die a little." It was a pleasant death.

This was the time when we began to think, not too seriously, about what we should do next. How long should we stay on the island? Should we plan to stay indefinitely, or only as long as our supplies lasted—some six months longer. And if we did decide to move away, where could we go and how could we get there?

Much as we stirred and turned these questons, we could come

to no definite decision. After all, we had no choice. Regardless of our plans or wishes, we would have to stay on the island until some kind of transportation turned up. What would turn up, and where would it be going?

An Ecuadorian ship? Not likely, but remotely possible. Ecuadorians did come to Santiago perhaps once a year, though not all Ecuadorian ships could give us transportation—they would either be overloaded already or they would be out of provisions. A tuna ship? There was probably our best chance. Some of the Good Manuels and Good Joes had indicated that they would be willing, even glad, to take us to San Diego. This method of travelling appealed to us, though we were not yet ready to go back to California. However, perhaps no tuna ships would come for several months—the fishing season was in abeyance too. We had not seen even a "Light-ho" since early in May. Another possibility was the tug boat from the base. A letter to the commander—but how could we mail it? The base was something like fifty miles away, but a letter might take months to reach it. Well, we would wait and see.

Waiting was not unpleasant, and we were in no hurry. Most of our troubles were also in abeyance. The wars were over. No need any more to fight against heat, torrents of water, insects, or even against hallucihorrors. Our diet, too, after long months of custom, now seemed quite satisfying. Our minds and bodies had become adapted to Santiago.

One more happy development added to our serenity. Just above the first water-hole Ainslie had discovered another outlet which yielded a good dozen gallons a day. How long the new hole would continue to produce, was, of course, on the knees of the gods. But we had to trust the owners of those knees, having little else to trust, and that too was a load off our shoulders.

It occurred to me that just then we had everything the Lord's Prayer asks for—in reasonable measure, though I have no doubt that the Lord had reasonable measure in mind. Daily bread, forgiveness of sins—having no one to sin against, we needed no forgiveness—deliverance from temptation and evil. Most of us, including ourselves, ask for a good deal more, but the essentials are covered by the paternoster. We could live on those essentials for—well, another year perhaps.

Oh, sure, there were times when I wished so fervently for an all-white, brand-new, paint-and-enamel kitchen that I actually smelt fresh paint where I should have smelt fish guts and goat manure. At other times I planned new clothes and other feminine fripperies—I even vowed to paint my toe-nails for the first time in my life the very next chance I had. (Incidentally, two years after leaving Santiago, I have no white enamel kitchen and I have not yet painted my toe-nails.)

Ainslie could have been quite happy if he could have found a cigarette tree, and, as a sort of extra-special Santa Claus gift, a twenty-pound Swift's Premium Ham. However, forget everything else and take two-thirds of Santiago Island for a steady, unfailing supply of tobacco! No help for his problem in the Lord's Prayer—that prayer had been invented too early and in the wrong place. Ainslie was led into temptation—temptation to curse his nerves and the innocent *chala* that could not manufacture nicotine.

"For a plugged *sucre* I'd cross the lava and ask Hitler if he has any cigarettes," was his feeble, daily jest.

Hitler was still with us in other ways too, always stealing or hiding things. Once he really seemed to have got away with something. Ainslie had caught and tied up a goat on his way back from the spring one morning, and in the evening he went to butcher it. In ten minutes he returned.

"That Hitler again!" he said. "He got my goat."

"You mean the goat or your goat?"

"The goat. She was gone, rope and all. And I can't see how, for I tied her up with a slip-proof knot. Not a single goat has untied my knots before. Must have been Hitler."

We could not think of a satisfactory explanation. The goat's escape was annoying, but it was something to wonder about, and Ainslie forgot for a few hours that *chala* is not tobacco.

The next day was Sunday, the last in June. It started as an exceptionally bad day for Ainslie. His tobacco craving came in waves; not too bad one day; very, very bad the next. The morning had one pretty highlight, which helped for about five minutes. A dozen pink flamingoes flew in V-formation high over El Corral on their way to the salt lake. They looked like pink crosses, the long legs and neck making the horizontal piece. We took delight in seeing them—something we had missed from the island scene was coming back home.

"I wonder if flamingoes are birds of good or ill omen," I said.

"Must be bad," was Ainslie's glum opinion. "Nothing good can happen today—I feel too horrible. Anyway, it's Sunday, and in all the time we have been here, nothing special has ever happened on Sunday."

Usually we went fishing or exploring on Sunday afternoon, but this time Ainslie felt that he needed something more strenuous to discipline his nerves. Though the road was completed and more work on it only a sort of perverse luxury, Ainslie set himself to trimming the edges and burning dead brush. To his odd way of thinking, this was recreation, though to the innocent bystander he might have looked like a rock-pile convict, travailing sadly and grimly.

With Ainslie out of the way, I took the opportunity to examine our food supplies for signs of spoilage or infestation and poured out all the beans and rice on sheets spread in the sun. Then I washed and sunned the containers—some twenty five-gallon gasoline tins, the only insect and moisture proof containers we had been able to purchase in Guayaquil.

I had started the tedious job of putting the supplies back in the cans when I became aware of a humming sound. It reminded me of a plane, but so convinced was I too that nothing special could happen that day—nothing special had happened for two months—that I did not even raise my head to look. "It is only the wind blowing across the top of the tin," I told myself.

In a minute I knew that a plane was coming. Those who really listen to planes can tell when one is coming, not just passing —there is a sort of purposeful tone to the increasing volume of sound. I ran up the nearest hill.

A bomber was on the way in again from the direction of the base. Ainslie had seen it and was coming toward the beach at a trot, the dog running ahead of him excitedly. She had learned that the sound of a motor was connected with visitors—nice men who patted her and gabbled baby-talk, which just filled her dish.

Ainslie put a match to a pile of brush. Frantically we pulled grass and weeds to make a better smoke, for the plane was circling to lose altitude. "They're going to drop mail again," we kept repeating.

The flyers were coming in low now, right over the fire, and a little white sack with a yellow streamer hit me on the toe. I was wearing a bright red sweater, which may have attracted the eye of the bombardier.

Ainslie's hands shook so that he could not open the bag. He just waved to congratulate the flyers, who spiralled upward again and out over the bay, but did not go away as they had done when they brought mail the first time. They returned to circle over the island.

After a struggle with the strings I had the bag open and shook out the contents—a handful of pebbles and a folded sheet of typing paper. On the paper was typed in telegraphic capitals:

"MR. AND MRS. CONWAY: U.S. TUG 843 WILL BE ARRIVING YOUR ISLAND APPROXIMATELY 5 PM LOCAL TIME, FOR PURPOSES OF EVACUATION, DUE TO THE FACT THAT THREE PRISONERS HAVE ESCAPED FROM VILLAMIL PRISON CAMP. THE PRISONERS ARE THOUGHT TO BE HEADED IN THE DIRECTION OF YOUR ISLAND."

Both of us read the message aloud, not able in a moment to take in the full meaning. There is such a thing as being stunned by news. "This is so sudden," was all I could think of saying.

Then Ainslie said something I had not yet thought of. "That goat. Perhaps Hitler is innocent, after all. The convicts got it. A fat doe, securely tied to a tree, would be a godsend to those desperate, starving bastards. They couldn't run a goat down without a dog. They are all diseased and half-dead."

"Not so dead if they escaped by sea to Santiago!" I reminded him.

There was scarcely time to jitter belatedly at the thought that we had slept innocently and peacefully through the night with three desperados loose on the island. A phrase in the message hit us between the eyebrows: "5 PM LOCAL TIME." That would be in two hours, and perhaps the tug would have to return to the base as soon as we could get on board.

We started down the hill, where we had been standing in a daze, and turning toward camp we happened to look seaward. There was the tug already, fussily churning the sea and within minutes of reaching the bay. No time for anything more than to take up the beans and rice I had forgotten and change into something presentable before we went down to the beach to meet whoever might came ashore.

The tug anchored, but for half an hour no one landed. Meanwhile the plane kept circling and dropped a few flares—we could not guess what for.

The young captain in charge of the evacuation was in the first landing boat with the tug commander, who turned out to be one of Ainslie's friends of the base-building days.

"I'll forgive you for what you are doing to us, Bill," said Ainslie as he shook hands, "if you will give me a cigarette."

While the commander fumbled in the pockets of the sweater and the heavy coat he was wearing, three other hands were extended with opened packs, each of a different brand.

"It's an ill wind——" I started to quote.

"That it is," agreed the commander, as he pulled the coat closer across his chest.

The captain hastened to interrupt these irrelevancies—he had a mission on his hands. He explained, as if reciting a lesson, that the Ecuadorian *comandante* at the base had received a radio message warning him that the Villamil prisoners had escaped seaward. Immediately the *comandante* had remembered the two *gringos* alone on Santiago, and become acutely conscious of his moral responsibility. "*Dios mío*," he had exclaimed, "this could lead to serious international complications!" He had dashed up to ask the commander of the American contingent to send a rescue mission on behalf of his fellow-countrymen, who were in great danger—if not already beyond human aid.

On his own part the captain added inducements. We would be taken to the base where I could talk with other women—all two of those present at the time—and where we could see movies and drink an occasional bottle of beer. He thought that after our long exile we might really enjoy a spot of civilised cheer.

"You don't need to sell the base to us," I chattered, not knowing what else to say. "We'll go willingly and not try to resist the U.S. Air Force. That outfit has had too much experience lately taking islands."

Ainslie was too occupied smoking and telling the invaders about the missing goat to say anything about willingness. My guess was that he was not willing, and in the back of his mind he was scratching vainly for methods to put off the evacuation.

The story of the goat was a sensation, though not all of our rescuers were equally convinced that the convicts could have reached the island. We had our own doubts; but *¿quién sabe?* Things like that had happened before in the Galápagos. The convicts had nothing but life to lose in making the attempt, and the life was forfeit, anyway.

The plane kept on searching for another hour, and in the second landing-boat were three sergeants armed as if for an invasion. No one but ourselves was taking any chances.

The others stopped at El Corral to talk, but the three rifle-packing sergeants immediately took off toward the spring to look around. If any convicts were on the island, all the to-do must have put them on their guard. We were among those who did not expect the searchers to find anything out of the way.

Soon the captain and his lieutenant let their curiosity get the better of their caution and said they would look around, too. Ainslie, armed with his twenty-two, went with them. I was left alone in camp with Commander Bill. He was heavy set and said he did not feel like man-hunting.

We sat under the *aromos* and talked. Casually, as if to relieve himself of the weight of it, Bill took out his pistol and laid it

on the table. Beside it he lined up a dozen cartridges, chatting the while about Panama and other irrelevancies we had in common.

In about an hour we heard men's voices. Bill picked up his pistol, but still as if it were casually. But I had caught on. He had remained in camp to "guard" me, and the business with the gun had not been playing. I felt at once important and silly, as if I were to blame for what was going on. In a way I was to blame, I decided. If it had not been for me, a fool woman on a fool desert island, the rescue mission might not have been sent. Ainslie alone could have been judged capable of taking care of himself—and, anyway, had I not consented to go with him, he would not have been on Santiago either.

The approaching voices were Ainslie's and the young officers'. They had not seen anything worth reporting. The other searchers had scattered farther out, perhaps to hunt goats, since as yet they had not found more exciting game.

A dozen more men came ashore from the tug. Among them were two of the Angermeyer brothers from Santa Cruz, who had happened to be at the base when the tug left and had come along for the excitement. Several of the newcomers, including the Germans, went goat-hunting. The commander had ordered his mission to bring back game as well as evacuees and prisoners. Others began knocking down doves with sticks, for which sport I was the instructor. The evacuation business was turning into a picnic.

By sunset four dressed goat carcasses were hanging on nearby trees, and fifty doves had been killed and prepared for barbecuing. The boys made two immense fires for a good supply of coals. "What will the convicts, if they are present, think of them?" I wondered. A couple of the tug's crew who came in after dark said that from the ship it looked as if the island were on fire.

One of the two Texans among the gun-toting sergeants was an excellent barbecue chef. We knew Galápagos doves were good to eat, but were now surprised to learn how good. Emergency rations that the soldiers had brought along were eaten only because there were not enough doves. Being Galápagans in good standing, the Angermeyers put in some good work on my braised goat, which I had seasoned with some of the barbecue sauce.

Nobody wanted to go to bed. But the tug commander reminded the crowd that he would have to be back at the base by noon the next day, and we had not yet had a moment for packing, which was a big task. Bed it had to be, if for only a few hours.

Some went aboard the tug, others preferred to sleep ashore. We broke out some mats and blankets for the Angermeyers, who elected to sleep in the *patio*. The sergeants, fully armed, went up the hill behind El Corral with mattresses they had brought from the boat.

We did not sleep much. Excited with so much good company, the dog barked all night, and the sergeants on the hill kept shooting the breeze until morning. Nothing tremendous happened.

At breakfast-time Sergeant "Red" Collins, another Texan and a good story-teller, said that the night had not been quite so uneventful as we had thought.

"You know we were sitting up there on the hill, and maybe around two o'clock we heard footsteps. They'd come a little way, then stop, and come on again. We lay down, right quiet, with our guns at the ready and pointing in the direction where the footsteps were coming from. We waited, all keyed-up and breathless, but nothing showed. Soon we could hear no more footsteps. There was silence for a long time.

"Then there was a sort of huff behind us. We had forgotten to guard our rear. I turned in no time flat, and was ready again. Still I saw nothing. 'Cautious bastards they are,' I thought.

"Pretty soon came a sound like someone walking up very, very easy. I thought I heard breathing. 'Now,' I said to myself, 'something is going to happen.'

"As I pinned my eyes on the skyline, two dark shapes, standing straight up, came over the brow of the hill. The shapes moved, and my finger twitched on the trigger. But I did not shoot, not quite yet. 'In another second,' I thought.

"Two more shapes appeared over the hill. Then a third pair, just like the first two. I let out my breath and relaxed my finger. 'Do you see what I see?' I asked the other guys.

"'Doggone jackasses!' said Sergeant Mills. 'If I were not sure they belong to Conway, I'd shoot.'"

The three sergeants, Collins said, had been chosen for their task because they were the best shots at the base.

"Too bad you had to waste your skill guarding us from burros," I said.

"Don't know about that. We still don't know if the prisoners are here or not. With all these people ashore, they wouldn't show up. They'll come sneaking around after we leave. In a few days we'll come back to see if there are any signs."

Ainslie told the captain that we would not break up the camp or take away anything but our clothing, the chickens, the dog, and all tools with cutting edges. We would leave El Corral "buttoned up," as he put it, the food and other things stored in the oildrums and boxes, and the entrances to the corral barred with large sandstone slabs. On our return, which we expected to be in a few days, we would decide what to do about breaking camp. Privately Ainslie hoped that the excitement would blow over and we could come back to Santiago for an indefinite stay. We were not yet ready to call the adventure finished.

With this and that, the tug was not ready to pull out until noon, and it was getting dark when we were jeeped five miles across the red Baltra flats to the American base headquarters. We were given an abandoned officers' barracks to live in—our choice of four rooms, all alike and furnished with cots and bedding. Snooping around, the first thing I found was a bobby pin. Visiting Wacs from the Canal Zone had been guests in the place a couple of weeks previously.

During breakfast of canned orange juice and creamed beef on toast the next morning, the commanding officer, an amiable West-Virginian, hoped that we would stay at the base over the Fourth, which was only a week away. "We'll have a barbecue and free beer," he offered as inducements. Naturally we were grateful, but feared that we ought to get away sooner.

Not only did we stay to show no mercy on the memorable Fourth of July barbecue, to which the Ecuadorian naval personnel, quartered on the beach at the former U.S. Naval Base, were also invited, but we were still on Baltra two months later. The tug, according to report, had been too busy to make the trip back to Santiago.

By that time we had decided not to try staying on Santiago again—which, we suspected, had been the object of the delay. The presence of two unprotected *gringos* on that hexed island, under existing circumstances, was, no doubt, too much for the Ecuadorian *comandante*'s peace of mind. And either to persuade us or because such a move was actually planned, the *comandante* told us in confidence that his government would soon establish a convict camp on Santiago. The colonists at Villamil were afraid of living so close to a group of desperate criminals who were constantly trying to escape and often succeeding. Not until we had indicated that we were reconciled to settling tentatively on San Cristóbal did the tug commander receive orders to get our possessions from Santiago and transport us and them to Puerto Chico.

A plane, sent to reconnoitre and to give some visiting brass from the Canal Zone an outing, added pomp and circumstance to the tug's second invasion of James Bay. By the time we landed, all of us were tense with expectation. Had the convicts been around? And if they had, what would we find?

Ainslie and the commanding officer, who had come along for the adventure, were the first to reach our gate. It was still blocked just as Ainslie had left it. A pile of firewood beside it was intact.

"They have been here!" Ainslie exclaimed, as he cleared out the sandstone slabs. "Look!"

The *patio* was knee-deep in crumpled newspapers, which we recognised as our packing paper. All the boxes and cans had been opened and the lids thrown aside. Three empty cigarette cartons were on the bedroom floor, which was littered with match ends and enough butts to have made glory hallelujah for us two months ago.

A quick examination showed that none of the food was missing, and though the dishes and other household articles were everywhere but where we had left them, they too were all present. In fact, I found more food than we had left. On my bed was a large carton, containing what had once been bread, pie, and cookies, but were now mouldy weevils' nests.

"Ah, I see!" Ainslie said, as he checked the packing-boxes. "My tools! They are all gone. Now who could have wanted those and nothing else?"

"And my mirror," I added. A good, eighteen-inch mirror I had never looked into had been dug out from the very bottom of a box.

With an escort of armed soldiers Ainslie made a quick trip to the spring. He found that donkeys had pushed aside the sheet of roofing and the rocks covering the hole. No other signs of visitation were evident.

In the meantime I had reconnoitred the garden behind the house. All the papaya seedlings, which had been a foot high when we left them, had been neatly removed. Not by animals, for there were no tracks and animal looters do not bother to dig large holes to avoid breaking the roots.

We all became sleuths and concluded that there had been two groups of visitors—those who had left the food and the cigarettes, probably tuna fishermen, and those who had smoked the cigarettes and stolen the tools. The identity of the latter remained the unsolved element in the mystery. Hitler again?

On the way from Baltra, feeling optimistic, we had expected to load our goods directly on the tug and be gone by evening, but now there was a spirit-breaking task of packing and cleaning up to do. We had an obsession about the cleaning, for we could not leave El Corral in a mess—it meant too much to us. It had been our home, and we had built it with our own sweat and curses out of materials the desert had provided. We might never see the place again, but other people would, and for years afterwards it would be known as the Conways' place. By evening

I was so weary that for three nights in succession I dreamed of packing those boxes over again.

But when it was all done, we had feasting and celebration for free. A dozen enthusiasts had prepared a dove barbecue to end all dove barbecues. Once again barbarous bonfires lighted up the white trunks of *palos santos* in a circle of five hundred yards. This time there was beer and the company of old friends of two-months' standing. Among others, we had with us the mess sergeant and his wife, both Texans, and, of course, Sergeant Collins. A dove-eating contest between Ainslie and the mess sergeant resulted in a draw—eighteen birds apiece. Sergeant Collins was determined to keep the fires burning all night, and only the threat of force persuaded him to be a good boy and seek the company of his mattress.

In the morning the tug's crew helped Ainslie carry his worldly goods on board. Before he made his last trip with a load of roofing Ainslie piled up a generous legacy of firewood for the chance visitor who might need it. He wanted to leave El Corral with his blessing on it.

Presently one of the negroes of the crew came to see if there was anything left to carry away. There was nothing more.

"What's the matter?" he asked me, as I stood in the middle of the *patio* wondering if we had forgotten anything, and, as I have so often done before on leaving a place to which I do not expect to return, taking a last look around.

"Nothing," I answered.

"You look sad."

"No, I am only tired."

"I know that. I'll make the fire burn up. A fire is cheerful."

He piled some of Ainslie's wood on the coals until the flames licked the *muyuyu* limbs. "I sure love a fire," he said.

We watched the flames, he in a trance of admiration, I because I was afraid the tree would catch.

When the fire had burned down, the negro walked to the beach, and Ainslie came to bar the gate.

"O Beulah Land, sweet Beulah Land," the negro was singing, "upon your highest mound I stand, and look across the shining sea——"

Why was he singing that?

Before the tug pulled out of Puerto Chico late that afternoon, having left us and our belongings on the beach, an officer handed Ainslie and me two beautiful documents. One conferred on each

of us the "Super Royal Order of Hyperterrestrial Hoppers."
The other read as follows:

"To all who shall see these presents, greetings:
This is to certify that Elmer Ainslie Conway (or Frances
Conway) being of good health and sound mind, and of his
own volition with practically no duress did pass a period
of at least three suns, subjected to the vicissitudes of fickle
nature, in constant danger of the most treacherous flora and
the most loathsome fauna. In so doing he does qualify for
the fraternity of The Ancient and Honourable Order of
Goat Whiskered Galápagans. He will be rudely treated
accordingly, publicly shunned and avoided from this day
hence. Done by my hand this 28th day of August, 1947.
Signed, Keeper of the Herd."